Web-based Learning

Web-based Learning

Hemlata Talesra
Wasef Marashdeh
M L Nagda

AUTHORSPRESS

In association with

Rajasthan Council of Educational Administration and Management (Affiliated to Commonwealth Council of Educational Administration and Management)

Worldwide Circulation through Authorspress Global Network
First Published 2003
[illegible] Edition 2005
Reprinted 2007
by Authorspress

E-35/103, Jawahar Park
Laxmi Nagar, Delhi-110092

e-mail: authorspress@yahoo.com

Typeset in NewCenturySchlbk by Chitra Computers

Web Based Learning
ISBN 81-7273-228-7

Printed in India at Tarun Offset, Delhi.

Preface

Globalisation is a thought premise which demands innovation and implementation. 'Knowledge person' and 'knowledge capital' are predominant usages defining the requirements of future vision of mankind. Whether it be the constructivism or behavioursim or the psychophysical approach for the growth and development of personality which defines the dynamic learning premises, all have lulled the teacher and the taught and have got them closer if not physically, then intellectually.

Here web-based learning counts to much expected initiatives in terms of learning of the concrete and abstract of the known and the unknown. The explosion in the magazine of information technology has made it easy, and web-based learning has become an impressive outcome.

Learning culture and learning friendly environments develop a variety of skills, abilities, competence and problem-solving capacities in an individual and enhance interactive learning environments for systematising self-learning systems. Computer-mediated communication, web-based simulations and world wide web, mobile learning, e-learning and computer-assisted instruction add effectively to virtual learning. This publication elaborates all these premises in eight chapters—changing faces of learning environments, technology in web-based learning, web-based pedagogical learning, web-based teaching, interface design in computer-mediated classes, resource support in hitech learning, evaluation of web learning and management of web education. The multidimensional expression with organised and systematic presentation will lead the reader to grasp the content and effective applications management, accomplishing the desired objectives of transforming, performing, confirming and resistant orientations. This publication deals with cognitive, affective and psychomotor domains equally well.

It is no more a misnomer that education is moving away from the traditional schedules and processes of instructions to an emphasis on student learning, and learning is a result of construction, collaboration, reflection and negotiation within a rich context in which learning is situated. Web-based communications technology not only offer supplement for traditional delivery methodologies, but also as being capable of revolutionising distant teaching and bringing on-and-off-campus teaching modes closer to alignment. Lifelong learning, learner-directed learning, learning to learn, contextualised learning, customised learning, transformative learning, collaborative/cooperative learning and just-in-time learning and all other educational requirements require to be web-based, computer-based and instructor-based, and learning content management systems enhance the knowledge premise of learners. This publication nicely elaborates this. For readers this book proves a guiding principle for web-based learning.

Editors

Contents

1

Changing Faces of Learning Environments

Educational use of Information and Communication Technologies (ICTs) have made an enormous contribution to improving education and to the development of learning theories. Increasing competitiveness, technological change and the re-engineering of production and social processes require continuous upgrading of skills and personal growth. Technological innovation, the adoption of new teaching/learning theories and social change all call on teachers to modify their role, to introduce new contents, tools and methods, and to deal with a heterogeneous student population.

Increased competitiveness and the resulting need to improve and diversify the training they offer means that trainers must have theoretical and practical know-how in new techniques for delivering training. This in turn calls for the application of new methods for presenting contents and organising learning activities. Another area strongly affected by change is that of private companies, especially small and medium enterprises.

Market globalisation and ever fiercer competition call for highly trained, highly efficient staff who are able to make a constructive contribution towards innovation in methodology and contents. A further example lies in public administration. Public demand for greater efficiency and upgraded services requires personnel with the flexibility to adapt to new roles and the capacity to adopt information technologies to meet that demand. These situations entail a shift away from the traditional study-work sequence; the formation of one's cultural background is no longer something that can be encapsulated within schooling alone, but must be spread throughout one's whole working life.

Sporadic in-service training courses delivered in short spurts in fixed locations without specific tailoring cannot possibly meet individual learning needs. What is more, they impose time restrictions that clash with production requirements and have a low cost/benefit ratio, thus representing only a partial response to training needs. The potential that multimedia and network technologies offer for the development of individual learning skills within four different adult populations: teachers, trainers, company employees and public servants.

LEARNING THEORIES

Constructivism

Constructivism is a learning philosophy. Learning is a search for meaning. Therefore, learning must start with the issues around which students are actively trying to construct meaning. Meaning requires understanding wholes as well as parts. Therefore, the learning process focuses on primary concepts, not isolated facts.

The purpose of learning is for an individual to construct his or her own meaning, not just memorise the "right" answers and regurgitate someone else's meaning. Since education is inherently interdisciplinary, the only valuable way to measure learning is to make the assessment part of the learning process, ensuring it provides students with information on the quality of their learning.

Constructivism calls for the elimination of a standardised curriculum. It promotes using curricula customised to the students' prior knowledge. Also, it emphasises hands-on problem solving. Under the theory of constructivism, educators focus on making connections between facts and fostering new understanding in students.

Instructors tailor their teaching strategies to student responses and encourage students to analyse, interpret, and predict information. Teachers also rely heavily on open-ended questions and promote extensive dialogue among students. Constructivism calls for the elimination of grades and standardised testing.

Behaviourism

Behaviourism is a theory of animal and human learning that only focuses on objectively observable behaviours and discounts mental activities. Behaviour theorists define learning as nothing more than the acquisition of new behaviour. Behavioural or operant conditioning occurs when a response to a stimulus is reinforced.

Behaviourism does not account for all kinds of learning, since it disregards the activities of the mind and does not explain some learning—such as the recognition of new language patterns by young children—for which there is no reinforcement mechanism.

This theory is relatively simple to understand because it relies only on observable behaviour and describes several universal laws of behaviour. Its positive and negative reinforcement techniques can be very effective—both in animals, and in treatments for human disorders such as autism and antisocial behaviour. Behaviourism often is used by teachers, who reward or punish student behaviours.

Brain-based Learning

This theory is based on the structure and function of the brain. As long as the brain is not prohibited from fulfilling its normal processes, learning will occur. Traditional schooling, however, often inhibits learning by discouraging, ignoring, or punishing the brain's natural learning processes.

Teachers structure learning around real problems, encouraging students to also learn in settings outside the classroom and the school building. Since all students are learning, their assessment should allow them to understand their own learning styles and preferences. This way, students monitor and enhance their own learning process.

Designers of educational tools must be artistic in their creation of brain-friendly environments. Instructors need to realise that the best way to learn is not through lecture, but by participation in realistic environments that let learners try new things safely.

Learning Styles

The learning styles theory is based on research demonstrating that, as the result of heredity, upbringing, and current environmental demands, different individuals have a tendency to both perceive and process information differently. The different ways of doing so are generally classified as:

i) *Concrete and abstract perceivers*: Concrete perceivers absorb information through direct experience, by doing, acting, sensing, and feeling. Abstract perceivers, however, take in information through analysis, observation, and thinking.

ii) *Active and reflective processors*: Active processors make sense of an experience by immediately using the new information. Reflective processors make sense of an experience by reflecting on and thinking about it.

iii) *Traditional schooling tends to favour abstract perceiving and reflective processing*: Other kinds of learning are not rewarded and reflected in curriculum, instruction, and assessment nearly as much.

Educators must place emphasis on intuition, feeling, sensing, and imagination, in addition to the traditional skills of analysis, reason, and sequential problem solving. Teachers should design their instruction methods to connect with all four learning styles, using various combinations of experience, reflection, conceptualisation, and experimentation. Instructors can introduce a wide variety of experiential elements into the class-room, such as sound, music, visuals, movement, experience, and even talking.

Observational Learning

Observational learning, theory, occurs when an observer's behaviour changes after viewing the behaviour of a model. An observer's behaviour can be affected by the positive or negative consequences—called vicarious reinforcement or vicarious punishment—of a model's behaviour.

There are several guiding principles behind observational learning, or social learning theory. Learning by observation involves four separate processes: attention, retention, production and motivation.

a) *Attention*: Observers cannot learn unless they pay attention to what is happening around them. This process is influenced by characteristics of the model, such as how much one likes or identifies with the model, and by characteristics of the observer, such as the observer's expectations or level of emotional arousal.

b) *Retention*: Observers must not only recognise the observed behaviour but also remember it at some later time. This process depends on the observer's ability to code or structure the information in an easily remembered form or to mentally or physically rehearse the model's actions.

c) *Production*: Observers must be physically and/ intellectually capable of producing the act. In many cases the observer possesses the necessary responses. But sometimes, reproducing the model's actions may involve skills the observer has not yet acquired. It is one thing to carefully watch a circus juggler, but it is quite another to go home and repeat those acts.

d) *Motivation*: In general, observers will perform the act only if they have some motivation or reason to do so. The presence of reinforcement or punishment, either to the model or directly to the observer, becomes most important in this process.

Human development reflects the complex interaction of the person, the person's behaviour, and the environment. The relationship between these elements is called reciprocal determinism. A person's cognitive abilities, physical characteristics, personality, beliefs, attitudes, and so on influence both his or her behaviour and environment. These influences are reciprocal, however.

A person's behaviour can affect his feelings about himself and his attitudes and beliefs about others. Likewise, much of what a person knows comes from environmental resources such as television, parents, and books. Environment also affects behaviour: what a person observes can powerfully influence what he does. But a person's behaviour also contributes to his environment. Educators must encourage collaborative learning, since much of learning happens within important social and environmental contexts.

Problem-Based Learning

The term 'problem-based learning' tends to be used to describe an approach to curriculum which is problem-centred rather than discipline-centred. The problem-based approach was developed in order to improve the quality of medical education by shifting from a subject and lecture-based curriculum to an integrated curriculum structured by 'real life' problems which crossed traditional discipline boundaries.

Problem-based learning is now used worldwide in higher education in areas such as architecture, computing, engineering, social work and business. While using problems as a stimulus for learning is not new and is used by many teachers to encourage student learning, for example, using case studies in tutorials, a problem-based curriculum is significantly different from the traditional subject-based curriculum. Features of a problem-based curriculum are as follows:

a) *Cumulative learning:* A subject is not learned indepth at any one time, but is introduced repeatedly and in increasing levels of complexity during the course of study.
b) *Integrated learning*: Subjects are introduced as they relate to a problem rather than separately.
c) *Progression in learning*: What and how students learn changes as students acquire skills and knowledge and as they mature.
d) *Consistency in learning:* The aims of problem-based learning are reflected in all aspects of teaching and learning, including the learning environment in the classroom and assessment practices.

Engagement Theory

Engagement theory is a model for learning in technology-based environments which synthesises many elements from past theories of learning. The fundamental idea underlying the engagement theory is that students must be meaningfully engaged in learning activities through interaction with others and worthwhile tasks.

While in principle, such engagement could occur without the use of technology, that technology can facilitate engagement in ways which are difficult to achieve otherwise. For example, with its emphasis on meaningful learning, it is very consistent with constructivist approaches. Since it emphasises collaboration among peers and a community of learners, it can be aligned with situated learning theories. Since it focuses on experiential and self-directed learning, it is similar in nature to theories of adult learning.

By engaged learning, means that all student activities involve active cognitive processes such as creating, problem solving, reasoning, decisionmaking, and evaluation. In addition, students are intrinsically motivated to learn due to the meaningful nature of the learning environment and activities.

The engagement theory is based upon the idea of creating successful collaborative teams that work on ambitious projects that are meaningful to someone outside the classroom. The collaborative learning suggests that, in the process of collaboration, students are forced to clarify and verbalise their problems, thereby facilitating solutions.

Collaboration also increases the motivation of students to learn, a significant consideration in settings with high dropout rates. Furthermore, when students work in teams, they often have the opportunity to work with others from quite different backgrounds and this facilitates an understanding of diversity and multiple perspectives.

The engagement theory is different from many older models of computer-based learning in which the emphasis was on individualised instruction and interactivity. It does promote interaction, but human interaction in the context of group activities, not individual interaction with an instructional programme. The latter form of interaction tended to be measured by single responses whereas engagement requires assessment of larger units of work. The difference between engagement and interactivity reflects the shift in thinking about computers in education as communication tools rather than some form of media delivery devices. Furthermore, the engagement theory places a great deal of emphasis on providing an authentic setting for learning, something not present in previous models.

Collaboration can be as simple as a two-minute in-class exercise involving pairs of students or as elaborate as a multiyear curriculum development project involving many teams. The classrooms are the most popular form of collaboration since they require minimal changes to the usual classroom routine. Laboratory science or fine arts make regular use of in-class collaboration, most courses do not. Yet collaborative learning is a technique that applies to any domain.

Email is one of the most important collaborative tools and it usually serves as the communication backbone for all activities. Web conference boards or chat programmes may also be important means for collaboration and sharing of results. The web will probably play an important role in terms of acquiring information. Students are also likely to make use of telephone conferences and fax communications, although these are not as convenient or cost-effective as online interaction.

In the future, desktop video may become popular as a means for inexpensive face-to-face interaction in a distributed learning environment. Since collaborative methods may be novel for many students and teachers, there is likely to be a high level of uncertainty at the beginning of such activities. Students will need guidance in working together including skills such as project management, scheduling, time management, leadership, consensus-building, etc.

Teachers will need practice in organising and conducting collaborative activities, particularly the facilitative role that is needed. A lot of attention has to be devoted to ways in which student teams can most effectively present and share their results with each other. And both students and teachers will need training and support in the use of all online communication tools.

For students who have jobs and work experience, it is a little easier since they can identify a project within their own organisation which is familiar to them. The instructor must screen all potential projects to ensure that they are appropriate for the subject matter involved and that the scope of work is feasible within the timeframe available. The instructor also serves as the student-client inference and must ensure that expectations are realistic for student projects completed in an academic context. Students have worked on campus related projects such as developing online systems for scheduling bus service and a television station, keeping records for a scuba club, designing a student ride board, organising car pools, and creating an accounting system for the physics department.

The teaching/learning activities of the classes were the same except that the electronic classroom students used a groupware programme for their collaborative learning exercises. A post-course questionnaire was used to measure students perceptions of their learning experience.

The technology-mediated collaborative learning resulted in higher levels of perceived skill development, self-reported learning, and utility than the traditional classroom. Furthermore, the test grades of the group of students who were in the electronic classroom were statistically higher than those of the groups of students in the traditional classroom.

The focus of engagement theory on meaningful and real-world learning activities is consistent with a more general trend in education. In short, the engagement theory represents a new paradigm for learning and teaching in the information age which emphasises the positive role that technology can play in human interaction and evolution.

DISTINCT LEARNING PROCESS

The learning process is one in which the student acts alone, even if physically he or she is with others. Studying by reading in one's own room or office is the protoypical example of learning by oneself. Learning is a process within a social context, in which more than one person may be present. The distinct learning process represented by four learning categories, representing different mixes of process activity and orientation. They are:

i) lectures,

ii) self-study,
iii) concurrent learning, and
iv) collaborative learning.

These learning categories are not mutually exclusive or superior or inferior to one another. They represent different approaches to individual and group needs and roles, addressing different stages in the integration of information into knowledge for the learner as an individual, and as a member of a social group.

In a traditional lecture in which a person talks while others listen, the student's activity is by oneself, while the orientation of the process is towards the group as a whole, i.e, the group-as-focus. Although the wish is frequently made that students interact more in this process, studies of student questioning reported that in the typical lecture situation, the frequency of questions per hour is only 3.0. Where this learning category demonstrates efficiencies is that a single person can place the same information within the reach of many.

This is the time-honoured way of utilising the scarce resources of experts, reaching back to a time when there was only an oral tradition of passing knowledge from one person to others. The lecture also has other potential strengths, including the ability to motivate others to certain behaviours, to inspire them to reflect deeply, or to perform logical analysis.

The learning activities in self-study are those performed by a person by himself. The process is also oriented to the person as the focus. Thus, solo reading, problem solving, individual experiments are typical of this category. However, some learning processes in this category could involve more than one person. For example, when a tutor is working with a student, the learning is being done by that student, and all the processes are also focused on the student. The technology support for self-study includes both electronic media as book, and as electronic tutor.

The learning activities in concurrent learning are in the character of being with-peers, in the sense that the activities involve learning together, through shared activities in a collegial manner. The processes are oriented around the person-as-focus, in that the goals and outcomes of the social and learning processes are individual in nature, rather than focused on the group as a whole.

The differences between concurrent learning and collaborative learning are the differences between the collection of goals of individuals, and the goals of a coherent collective culture, which can be viewed as an entity with its own measurable goals, achievements and outcomes.

The behaviour of both are based on with-peers activities, in other words, on collegial interactions. With concurrent learning, a group of peers interact to achieve their individual learning goals; with collaborative learning, a group of peers interact to achieve their collective learning goals.

In lectures, the individual is listening to the lecturer, in a passive rather than interactive way; the listener is the recipient, the lecturer is the active dispenser of knowledge. The listener is apart from others who may also be present, and in an interpersonal sense, they may as well not be present. The lecturer often is the source of authority that validates the process. Self-study is usually an individual activity, focused on internal cognitive processes. These learning activities often take place in the isolation of one's own room, office or laboratory. Where others are present, such as in a library, special social and interpersonal rules are established which provide virtual isolation.

The primary motivator for the self-study process is usually the student. A special situation of self-study in which another person is involved in a meaningful way is that of the tutor who works one-on-one with a student. The learning activities are all directed at the student's needs, and fit into the person-as-focus definition; there are no peers interacting with the student, and therefore the process orientation is also by oneself.

The interpersonal relationship with the tutor is an interactive one, where the tutor is in a sense, a dynamic extension of the knowledge to be acquired, providing guidelines, highlights, key strategies and motivation.

Concurrent learning describes situations in which a learner is interacting with peers, but the learning activities are individualised, rather than having a group focus. The nature of the interactions with others is that of exchanges of facts, opinions and values. There may often be a set of individual goals, rather than a common learning goal. Among common examples of concurrent learning are the seminar, classroom discussion, hallway or coffee chat at work. Included in this category are distributed interactions such as electronic forums, internet newsgroups and bulletin boards.

Thus, the style of interpersonal relationships may be competitive, confrontational or collegial, rather than consensus-reaching. It is not unusual for concurrent learning situations to have either formal or *ad hoc* referees, who facilitate the interactions and maintain them at a reasonable level of focus, interest and civility.

Electronic forums and bulletin boards use formal facilitators, while informal discussion groups find individuals taking on the role of the facilitator from time to time. The legitimacy of concurrent learning sessions are imbued as much in the general sense of acceptance of the process by the individuals, as in the existence and activities of the facilitators. The collaborative learning category describes situations in which a group of persons share common learning goals, and work together to achieve them.

Concurrent learning is a forum of individuals; collaborative learning is an environment in which each person attempts to be a coherent part of a whole, synthesising with one another a shared understanding of values as well as facts. The personal behaviours required of each person in such a setting are not necessarily intuitive or natural, and it is not uncommon for collaborative learning to be mediated and orchestrated.

The lecture environment constrains the listener to conform to the tempo of the lecturer's delivery, and to diverge from that sequence of ideas minimally. Learning in the self-study category is quite different. The student is in complete control of what is done next, mentally and physically. There is freedom to contemplate the relationship between two concepts, to explore a thought association, to work out something that was not being well understood. This self-directed environment requires discipline and focus, and for some persons who do not have this rigour, is an inefficient way of spending time and effort in learning.

The concurrent learning category is one in which the learning process is individually focused, while the activity is with peers. This environment is one in which many participants express their individual opinions, beliefs, and arguments, in an open forum in which the competing ideas of the persons involved shift into and out of focus.

The stimulation of receiving many different perspectives from others is offset by the inability to think much about any one thing before either getting another, or taking some action oneself. The environment is characterised by debate, and the validation or refutation of the arguments and supporting facts of the participants is very different from lectures and self-study.

In the collaborative learning paradigm, both learning focus and activity are oriented to the group. The individuals in the group work together to achieve common learning goals, arriving at a consensus. The environment is characterised ideally by sharing, openness, acceptance of the contribution of others, and the development of a cohesiveness in which each person becomes aware of the shared achievement of all.

In this sense, successful collaborative learning among team members in a company is "organisational learning", with the organisation having learned if its members have acquired shared knowledge and values in both a self-aware and a group-aware way.

The lecture is better-suited for guiding the learner to appreciate the framework of a subject, its key concepts and highlights, rather than to a detailed understanding. This is not to say that a lecturer is unable to lead the student, through a clear sequence of steps, to a more profound and deeper understanding of a specific concept than the learner could achieve by himself. In self-study, the learner follows his own personal initiative in working with the material. Whether reading a book, watching a video, doing exercises, writing, listening to a tape, the learner is in full control of what next to do or think about.

If a concept is not well understood, or sparks a link to a new idea, the learner can choose to pursue the issue further, to whatever extent is desired. This personally directed, potentially non-linear flow of internal events means that the learner can seek to achieve a mastery of the subject matter, in a way that is not possible in the lecture or the other interactive group-focused categories.

The kind of knowledge that is realisable is therefore not only factual, but also the associations, relationships, and use of these facts in linkages to the learner's existing knowledge contexts. For this reason, self-study, which includes reflection, assimilation, integration and association of new concepts, as directed by the learner, is essential to furthering a person's learning in most domains. Concurrent learning describes an environment in which individuals pursue their own learning goals while interacting with one another. The pace and tempo of this interaction is not determined by any one person, and therefore reflection and self-directed thinking is not the order of the day.

In collaborative learning, individuals work together to achieve common learning goals, which are often declared formally, but may also be implicitly assumed in the process. The consensus that leads to group decisions are based as much on an understanding of shared values as on the set of facts and rational constructs through which these values find expression.

Self-study is a learning process in which students work at their own pace to acquire, reflect upon and integrate knowledge. Technology support for this learning process enhances this in a number of ways. It can provide the student with more powerful representations of knowledge, such as sounds, videos, and images. More important, learners have the freedom to move in this multimedia knowledge space that is almost as powerful as the freedom of self-directed thought. Facts, ideas, opinions are no more than a few keystrokes or mouse-clicks away. Most of all, technology support can provide an interactive environment in which the learner can find support, guidance, and responsiveness that is close to what a human tutor offers.

In this way, a learner is able to focus on personal learning goals through a supportive, adaptive and guiding process, that is at the same time highly personalised. This kind of technological support for learning in the self-study process is highly empowering, promising large potential gains in learning effectiveness and efficiency. The technology support for concurrent learning has been directed at increasing the scope and power of the open forums in which these learning processes take place.

The relationships between the learner and the elements of the learning process is in two ways: first, the basis for the interactions in terms of social validation, and second, the nature of the learning categories in terms of group dynamics. For the learning process to be effective, the learner needs to believe that the process is a valid one. The structural relationship of the student to the learning category is therefore along two dimensions. The first is based on social validation, which leads to the second, based on empowerment.

The lecture is a learning process in which the student's basis for validation is the authority of the lecturer; this leads to the group dynamics of an autocracy. For self-study to be effective, the students must believe that it is a valid process for learning. This validation is based on self-respect. To the extent that the student has a strong sense of self-respect, the effort spent in self-study is associated with positive expectations; this leads to highly autonomous behaviours on the part of the student.

Individual Learning

Individual learning may be defined as the capacity to build knowledge through individual reflection about external stimuli and sources, and through the personal re-elaboration of individual knowledge and experience in the light of interaction with others and with the environment. In modern-day society, this capacity is demanded of practically everyone.

The rapid change brought about by innovation, increased levels of competition and the unsuitability of other forms of training all mean that this ability needs to be much more keenly developed than in the past. The requisites for individual learning are perception of a need, identification of an object (an objective) that may satisfy that need, and identification of a strategy for reaching that objective.

In some cases these requisites are immediate: consider a child who learns to walk and talk in order to achieve freedom of movement and communication; or, more generally, a person who needs to learn how to drive a heavy vehicle or to use a foreign language so that he can interact with others.

However, in situations like these the motivational factor is extremely high, the relationship between need and objective is immediately apparent, and the path to achievement is direct and clearly defined. Generally speaking, few people have an innate capacity for individual learning.

Often, the need is not immediately clear, and the effort involved in fulfilling that need means that less time and energy will be dedicated to gratifying tasks. Moreover, instead of directly pursuing the ultimate objective, it may be necessary to proceed by striving towards indistinct intermediate goals.

In the case of schools and companies, for instance, needs are not seen as personal because they arise out of requirements imposed from an external organisation that the individual only identifies with in a fairly loose manner. This is in stark contrast with the position of the self-employed or corporate management, whose capacity for self-training is a vital element in carrying out their activity. The environment in which one operates may also be adverse towards innovation and offers no incentive for personal growth.

Take public administration, for example, which has traditionally operated using approaches and means that have become outdated in society at large. Individual endeavours to keep up-to-date on matters related to one's work are implicitly discouraged by the impossibility of putting into daily practice what has been learned. In addition, the frantic pace of activity in modern society leaves little time for rethinking what one does in an effort to improve performance.

Identifying the objective, or means, for fulfilling a need is difficult as it calls for initiative in acquiring information and knowledge and then evaluating these both individually and with the help of others. Take, for example, the need to acquire technological skills in order to compete on the job market. This calls for careful evaluation of the type of skills that may be useful, involving activities like reading newspaper articles about technology, examining job offers and reflecting about personal knowledge.

Different kinds of mental activities must be brought into action in order to acquire problem solving abilities: observing, imitating, generalising, discovering, making mistakes, correcting, analysing (breaking down), summarising (laying out), modelling (from the concrete to the abstract), comparing, classifying and so on. Take, for example, a training organisation called upon to develop training paths that meet the standards the market currently demands. This involves a number of steps:

a) study of the organisation's position regarding the factors that influence the quality of training;
b) identification of the key areas to tackle,
c) comparison of the organisation's stance with its competitors;
d) determining what standard should be pursued in terms of both internal structure and market demand;

e) scheduling of the adjustment programme; and

f) deciding the approach for evaluating results.

Behavioural attitudes include flexibility, adaptability, self-regulation (self-evaluation, awareness, willpower, sense of responsibility and self-reliance) and social regulation (organisation and management). To take an example, consider a teacher who needs to improve his professional performance by adjusting to shifting social conditions. Italian schools are currently facing new problems related to the increasingly multicultural and multi-ethnic composition of the student population and to rising dropout levels.

These observations underline the fact that any project aiming to foster the development of individual learning must help people to recognise their personal needs, and encourage them to identify and put into practice behavioural strategies and methods that make it possible to identify the means for doing so.

Individual learning may be developed in two ways: through individual activity or collaborative activity. The former comprises study, individual reflection, reworking of ideas and concepts, and the building up of new knowledge on the basis of what is already known. On the other hand, collaborative activity may be pursued either in a formal learning setting, where different teaching models are adopted, or in an informal manner as an integral part of one's work (situated learning). ICT can play a supportive role in these activities.

A well-known example in personal activity is provided by hypermedia systems. When these are paired with the more promising new theories regarding the design of learning environments, they represent a means of knowledge acquisition that, by approaching a certain topic from a variety of directions, makes it possible to choose the most suitable path for studying. In addition, hypermedia systems offer individual learning paths that make the creation of knowledge an active and continuous process.

As far as collaborative learning is concerned, a number of studies have revealed the positive effects on individual learning brought about by the use of synchronous and asynchronous communication tools. The advantage lies in the possibility of accessing the experience of others and of collaborating with others in the creation of a shared product. An example is provided by the use of discussion lists in companies. The aim here is threefold:

a) to create a repository of information and experience that is accessible on an international level;
b) to permit employees to help one another; and
c) to exchange experience.

In the real world, learning needs are often perceived not at the point when they ought to be satisfied but further downstream. Diagnostic systems, microworlds and technology-based simulation systems can all be of enormous help in guiding the user to anticipate his/her needs, offering stimuli for indepth study of problems and assistance in reflecting about them. Having the opportunity to work on a problem outside of its normal setting is crucial for understanding what individual needs are called for.

Certifying training, this system features a diagnostic module that measures the quality of the training on offer according to a number of parameters: internal structure of the organisation, type of competition and the quality standard gap. It has a library of hypermedia information that provides documents on various procedures, case studies, and orientation material. Measurement of the training organisation's performance against quality standards is done through a set of questions put to the user about the state of his organisation, the purpose being to get him to think about specific aspects calling for attention and thus about shortfalls to be addressed. The information library represents an initial tool for considering those shortfalls in detail. Certifying training is currently being tested in about a dozen training organisations located in regions throughout Italy. It is used both on an individual basis and in the context of collaborative situated learning.

Lifelong Learning

The lifelong learning is becoming part of everyday life, in all sorts of contexts, in a variety of circumstances and for everybody at all stages in their lives. Where learning is concerned, this means shifting from those situations where it is mostly a minority or special kind of activity to ones in which, increasingly and happily, everyone integrates elements of learning into their lives. It means recognising and cherishing those processes devoted to the generation and renewal of all forms of 'intellectual capital', an devising appropriate mechanisms to measure and evaluate it.

Many people never get beyond the earnest, yet banal, view that education is generally a 'good thing', or the assertion that there is a simple and self-evident direct link between educational attainment and prosperity. Communication and information technologies (CITs) are successfully embedded into curricula in various educational institutions all over the world.

There are number of problems related to technological solutions for individual and life-long learning (LLL). Conditions for individual learning changes in centuries, and for centuries autonomous learning coexisting with instruction did not share the same space with it. A thorny path of cognition, without milestones, pointers, and guides, was not attractive for a mediocrity. Scarcity of information sources, language barriers, inaccessibility of science, and segregation of education prevents the raise of independent learners.

Technologies opened new horizons for individual learning, enabling mouse-click access to information resources, variety of learning tools, environments and services. Technological support for a learner is implemented both for traditional, instructor-guided and independent, self-directed learning. The first approach relies on adaptation of a learning technology system (LTS) to a user based on his learner model or profile. As a result of this adaptation, a learning content is shaped to learner needs, appropriate presentation mode and learning activities are selected for the user's learning style, and an individual learning path is arranged to optimise the learning process.

The learner's acquisition of knowledge and skills without external control are important in the lifelong perspective, although with the growing role of learning occurred outside of the traditional educational setting the value of self-directed learning increases. Original works on self-directed learning were inspired by the growth of adult education. They drew the attention of university teachers seeking new ways to engage the learners into a creative process of building their personal knowledge structures, and experimenting with the modifications of the roles and functions of a teacher and student, and the essence of their interaction.

Technologies are able to make it smoother by arranging an intelligent support for learning-related activities, thus they allow for natural embedding of the learning into a professional activity. A particular paradigm of learning may be represented as an optimisation task with a target function depending on a number of variables attributed to parameters of the learning process. In individual learning, the learning goals and content preferences are not uniform. One learner tries to maximise an amount of content or exercises for a given time, another seeks the most enjoyable way of learning.

Learning content may be studied indepth or surfed to evaluate the coverage of the resource. The priorities and criteria of an individual user are usually not reported to the LTS. Therefore, the developers of systems and tools prioritise certain features of their products at the expense of the others. For instance, in online dictionary design the priority is given to the convenient representation and retrieval of local information units referenced by their names.

The relations between these units and an opportunity to browse the related material presented in the dictionary is out of focus, although, for autonomous learning, these issues may be at least equally important. Thus, evaluating the same product from the lifelong perspective, the target function and the list of parameters should be reconsidered. One of the recent approaches related to lifelong learning, "just-in-time" (JIT), is aimed at enabling a learner to attain the required level of performance over current task by spending minimum time for training and learning. In skills-based training this approach allows for exercising newly acquired skills during the performance of authentic tasks, therefore, learning and real work are combined, so the learning outcomes are immediately embedded into practice. In complex domains, an effective performance requires expertise beyond skill level. Thus, a synergy of approaches is needed to promote a transfer of "quantity" of skills into a "quality" of performance.

An idea of electronic performance support system (EPSS) is built upon just-in-time training, putting an emphasis on the creation of the resource-based environment instead of arranging human support. A parameter to be maximised for EPSS is an access to necessary resources and help services, other parameters can be inherited from JIT approach. Considering the key issues to be addressed in LLL, one can mention the following:

i) the users of learning resources have different background, expertise, goals, and priorities, so examples and explanations must be oriented at the diverse user community;

ii) learners need freedom in activities and learning material selection, as well as an opportunity of flexible interaction with resource facilitating the construction and elaboration of their learning strategies;

iii) the units of a learning material must enable their flexible combination and independent study, provide information for selection and sequencing;

iv) the learners need an opportunity to acquire not only specific knowledge and skills, but also an overall learning experience, develop learning abilities and qualities necessary for effective autonomous learning.

Therefore, a distinctive feature of LLL-oriented systems is flexibility of their use, which may be manifested by means of different functions depending on specifics of individual learning activities. It is evinced in the presentation of the learning material and arrangement of the learning activities, in the team-based recommendations of the sequence of learning, in a variety of supported practices.

The value for a particular user is determined by the system's ability to facilitate his individual learning. To clarify the needs in support, let us consider recommendations for the instructor working with self-directed learners and study the primary activities of the autonomous learner.

The instructor's role in training adult learners may be characterised by the following list of imperatives: encourage, help, discuss, recommend, create conditions, provide some models and examples. Thus, instead of teaching in a classical sense, an instructor creates an environment for successful learning, assists learning, motivates and inspires. The only space for instruction is left in teaching the essential learning skills.

Technological solutions could follow the recommended practice to create a supportive environment for the individual learner. In autonomous learning, the traditional set of tasks performed by a learner is amplified by the tasks usually attributed to a tutor or supervisor. Whereas some instructional support and guidance may be obtained by participation in arranged courses, the most important part of learning management remains a learner's own responsibility. An individual learner must be able to perform a variety of activities to identify learning goals and recognise starting conditions of the learning process, namely:

i) to match a number of career opportunities to a personal profile, including professional expertise, general skills, attitudes and preferences, and evaluate discrepancies;

ii) to recognise the need of learning and determine the goal in some form;

iii) to audit current skills and knowledge in respect to desired goal, to evaluate chances and expenses of attaining the goal, reconsider the goal, evaluate intermediate steps.

During the learning, besides the typical learning activities, aimed at mastering new knowledge and incorporating it into a mental model, an individual learner performs also control, evaluation and monitoring functions. The list of these "meta-learning" activities includes:

i) determination of current status of one's knowledge in relation to a task under consideration;

ii) setting some learning objectives, describing the amount of the content that should be learned, procedures that should be mastered, etc.;

iii) search for appropriate information sources, tools, services;

iv) selection of the adequate units for learning, taking into account both external (technical, economic) and internal preferences and restrictions;

v) arranging necessary activities to practise the application of the newly acquired knowledge;

vi) monitoring and sequencing learning;

vii) assessment of one's own understanding.

There are different stages of learning process—orientation, selection, comparison, static and dynamic planning, knowledge and skills acquisition, self-assessment, and monitoring. An intelligent tool described there facilitates the acquisition of cognitive skills in domains where qualitative decisions and reasoning are preceded or justified by extensive numerical data analysis.

A cognitive apprenticeship tool facilitates a gradual progress by stepwise engagement of a learner into the process of performance of the authentic tasks. An effect of the cognitive apprenticeship is twofold. At a planning stage, i.e., during a creation of the problem-solving procedure, a learner can make use of hints or follow an expert's advice.

At an implementation stage, during actual problem solution, separate steps are checked by the system and may be performed automatically. This approach is remarkable in two respects.

i) It allows to apply a method of training similar to the one that works well in exercises aimed at simple skills formation—a choice of tasks "from simple to complex". Working with the tool, a learner focuses on particular steps in problem solution and his mastery is growing both in execution of particular steps and in handling the authentic tasks.

ii) A knowledge-based interactive environment creates a background for individual support and consulting, usage of flexible procedures in problem solving, and assistance in performance of a user-defined tasks.

Modern software tools tend to incorporate more and more services and options, which make them attractive and friendly for experienced users but pose significant obstacles to novices. Companies have to preserve a balance between professional training of their employees to help them cope with technology upgrade and tight production deadlines requiring focusing on knowledge and skills that could be immediately applied.

In complex software tools, a number of functions applied for a particular task is relatively small, therefore, the priorities in mastery of a set of functions become an important issue. The right sequencing of functions to be mastered enables one to incorporate new skills in one's "professional toolbox" and practise one's application while performing professional duties.

The following are the several objectives of learning:

i) raising awareness of employability skills as an initial state in a process of revision of one's own skills, knowledge and abilities;

ii) assistance in the evaluation of the personal and professional profile;

iii) planning of learning actions to attain the desired professional state.

Many students all over the world still do not realise that they will need to keep learning to succeed in their professional career, and their ability to recognise the gaps in their knowledge, plan necessary learning actions, evaluate the results of learning and revise their professional skills will determine their promotion opportunities.

Students realised that it is their responsibility to identify and locate the critical knowledge they need taking into account the professional context. They had stronger internal motivation driven by a perception of the situations where the acquired knowledge may be applied. Moreover, some of them may be born as lifelong learners, they willingly and skilfully enhance their expertise, and are able to control the process and learn from available sources in a number of ways.

Some requisites of the individual learning include perception of a need, identification of an objective, and implementation of a strategy for attaining the goal. The first two can be considered as some preliminary activities necessary to launch a learning process, and the last covers the learning itself. The instructional software designed to motivate teachers to master new technologies, raise their awareness of the quality standards and certification demands, and introduce the best practice examples for technology-enriched classroom activities.

Identification of an objective is often complicated by the lack of information and skills to search and obtain it, the inability to match one's own abilities and capabilities to requirements and prerequisites. Strategy implementation support is illustrated by tools containing multiple representation of the same learning content and a bank of learning activities for a user, enabling both experimental approach to knowledge construction and built-in instructional guidance to a new material.

The systematic lifelong learning can significantly help develop people's skills, orientations and confidence to navigate the many risks, uncertainties and ambiguities of contemporary life. It can constitutes a key resource in enabling people to participate in the shaping society and to take advantage of social change, rather than being its possible victims. The lifelong learning will depend upon promoting widespread and systematic changes of culture in the society. This is essential if the demand for learning throughout life is to be greatly increased, participation in learning is to be substantially widened and forms of provision are to be systematically diversified. This process of change will be greatly aided by the design and implementation of an imaginative, major national campaign to promote lifelong learning, in all of its aspects.

Without such changes in culture, many well-intentioned, and often well-resourced, initiatives risk failure and likely disappointment. It is also important to recognise that, just as cultural change will need to proceed on many different fronts, so too a variety of different learning cultures will need to be created.

There is no 'one best way' or universally applicable type of learning culture, irrespective of people's circumstances or the organisational or institutional settings they find themselves in. Learning cultures will work effectively when they properly reflect the circumstances and needs of the people involved and their various organisations and institutions, and suit their own practical priorities and desires. The public interest manifested in The Learning Age and the wide acclaim for its vision have been most encouraging.

For many people, the very phrase 'lifelong learning' itself is still puzzling or, at best, rather vague. As yet, the expression has not fired the imagination of the population at large, especially those not yet engaged in learning beyond school—at work, in the community, in their homes and families and in their leisure and recreational lives. To some people, the notion of 'lifelong' learning sounds more like a penal sentence or endurance test than an invitation to pleasure, achievement and progress.

There is already a large number of policy initiatives and arenas of intervention which either include a specific lifelong learning dimension or in which there is much scope to fashion a contribution from lifelong learning. Recognising this potential and drawing the various strands together to ensure effectiveness, focus and coherence constitutes a major task.

Although the process of creating a rich diversity of cultures of learning throughout the society has already begun, and there are encouraging signs in some quarters, in many respects there is so far only piecemeal and uneven progress. While this is understandable at the beginning of such a shift in cultures, it is not yet evident that there is full acceptance even at the heart of government of the value of including lifelong learning across a range of initiatives. Emphasis now needs to be given to each of the following potentially major influences upon the development of learning cultures, in every dimension of contemporary life.

The kind of fundamental shift in attitudes and behaviour we are seeking to achieve will require cultural changes at many levels, and this should be reflected in the design and focus of the campaign we advocate. First, the motivation and commitment of individuals to learn will need to be increased. Their involvement in lifelong learning should both come to reflect their interests and priorities and engage them in shaping and supporting their own learning throughout their lives. This radical shift in orientations and values will take time. For the young, it should begin in school, or even earlier. The school curriculum itself, and its methods of delivery, should be so designed as to stimulate a love of learning, develop children's skills of learning, to learn and be aimed at securing a commitment to learning throughout life from everyone.

For adults, the pleasures and uses of learning should be widely stimulated and imaginatively reinforced in their everyday lives and in the many environments in which they move—at home, in work, in their leisure pursuits and in the community. All of those institutions which provide learning—schools, colleges, universities and private bodies—will need to review and change their cultures and current ways of working.

Learning can take many forms, both formal and informal. It can include developing a variety of skills, abilities, competencies and problem-solving capacities. It quite properly includes acquiring new information and knowledge, as well as the pursuit of credits and qualifications through programmes of study more conventionally recognised as 'learning'.

The general barriers to increasing participation in adult learning so far identified include people's preference to make other use of their free time, pressures on time at home and work, location, finance, domestic and caring responsibilities, lack of information and absence of opportunity, a belief amongst many that learning has little to offer them and unhappy memories of school. The sources of learning, including communications and information technology, should be universal and should increasingly become a routine part of the organisational, cultural and physical environment of everyday lives.

Even the architecture and design of public spaces should come to include access to lifelong learning opportunities for all, including the availability of information and communications technology. The 'learning pays' for individuals, some kinds of learning clearly pays more than others, both materially and subjectively. Making use of the Campaign for Learning's typology of different potential learning environments draws attention to those which are either less obvious or even unexpected and yet in which access to learning could be facilitated and engagement increased.

Learning-friendly environments should be promoted by means of competitions and guidelines to encourage learning-friendly design for workplaces, public spaces, shopping centres and other buildings from architects and others; and developing planning regulations with incentives and requirements to include the creation of learning centres and access to communication and information technology. More potential consumers of learning should be reached by considering the use of giving additional credits on Individual Learning Accounts through supermarket 'loyalty cards' and on the basis of train or bus miles; and instituting weekly lottery prizes to cover the fee and maintenance costs of learning programmes.

INTERACTIVE LEARNING ENVIRONMENTS

Interactive learning environments allow different representations of the same situation and serve a twofold purpose: to improve student learning and to explore first-hand a number of different teaching/learning approaches, testing learning theories and uncovering new problems for investigation.

In this sense, interactive learning environments can represent the focus for training activities designed to stimulate teachers to update their practice. This is done by confronting them with new issues regarding their role, class dynamics, conceptions about the subject matter being studied, and learning difficulties, so that they are led indirectly to reflect about their individual behaviour in relation to these areas. A noteworthy example of such environments is provided by courses based on the microworlds concept and its exemplification.

In traditional education, the learner is rarely involved in the choice of the objective for satisfying the learning need, and this is one of the main factors behind the failure of many training programmes. ICT changes all this, helping people to perform both individual and social activities designed to control the objective through which the learning need may be satisfied.

In terms of personal activity, what comes to mind here are multimedia systems for self-learning, which make it possible to set the objective in a top-down manner: beginning with a very wide view of an issue, examining various facets separately, and concentrating on those deemed to be of special interest so that one particular aspect is singled out.

Self-learning systems can be greatly enhanced when used in tandem with web browsing. If carried out with a clear target in mind, web browsing develops the fundamental skills of learning to find and recognise sources of information, critically analysing and comparing them, and choosing those that are relevant to the problem at hand. As far as social activities are concerned, the importance of ICT lies in the greater possibilities for communication offered by the network, both in terms of the number of interlocutors available and the different types of communication available.

In today's tight job market, young people are forced to disregard their skills and interests when looking for employment, thus increasing their frustration and further limiting their chances of success. Job hunting is an activity that requires personal initiative and capabilities like setting objectives, deciding strategies, looking for useful information, and so on—qualities typical of individual learning. The tool helps the user to identify the kind of job that suits his personality best by describing various forms of employment, related legislation, the aptitudes required, and so on. It also encourages users to draw on the experience of others in order to clarify personal objectives. This is done by granting access to external information sources like employment agencies, employers' organisations and unions, databases, etc.

Experimental uses of the tool have produced very promising results: when asking for further help from those in the work orientation sector, users are submitting plans on how to move and are aware of their personal needs. In the light of its success, the tool can now be consulted in numerous public institutions in Italy. In many cases, however, it is difficult for teachers to get access to the results of projects engaged in by others because information about them is circulated within a restricted community. Collaborative environments permitting the sharing of information about didactic programmes and their re-elaboration provide the ideal answer to this problem.

The local network in the Genoa area created a Computer Mediated Communication (CMC) environment where teachers store their experiences, provide comments and observations on those of others, form work groups to discuss those experiences, and so on. The learning path through the environment demonstrates the gradual passage that both the groups of learners and the collaborative objects follow as they emerge from the blur and acquire ever greater clarity and articulation. ICT offers support in a number of ways when users are choosing a strategy that suits them: by making available a range of vastly different tools that can be used in the same environment; and by allowing the adoption of different approaches to the same topic using a single tool.

The tools in the former case cover a wide spectrum. This ranges at one end from educational planning environments that adopt a systematic and controlled approach in order to lighten the learner's burden and provide rapid feedback, to environments for knowledge organisation and representation that call on the user to take total control of resources. Some tools offer an individual pathway to knowledge building, others foster social interaction so as to develop collaborative learning, while still others combine both of these approaches. As to the multi-use tools, some of these feature multiple, inter-linked representations of the same knowledge, others combine computer activities with hands-on experiments and observation, while still others allow the adoption of different learning strategies in accordance with the path, learning period and level of study that the user sets.

The office automation training that company staff receive in Italy usually focuses on technical explanation of systems, rather than demonstrating through practical examples the impact these systems may have on the way everyday tasks are carried out. What's more, training rarely takes into account personal aspects like technophobia, fear of being shown up in front of colleagues, and lack of technical background. Taking these ideas as a stating point, we have developed a package of multimedia material called CBT-Office Automation.

The material allows the user to adopt different learning strategies, such as learning through examples, problems, theoretical explanations or self-evaluation, according to the length and level of study that the user chooses. In addition, learning is contextualised because the contents are learned by applying them in order to solve real probiems. Furthermore, the material can be exploited in two different ways. On the one hand it can be used autonomously for studying concepts, learning to tackle problems individually or for formulating hypotheses and verifying them.

A multimedia system analyses the conceptual difficulties involved in several mathematical topics, proposes keys for interpreting those problems and suggests questions to examine when designing activities to overcome them. The problem of comparing the different interpretations, answering the questions, and relating the activities to classroom teaching is left to the teacher. The system was tested with about 40 teachers in various regions of Italy: the results were encouraging in that teachers demonstrated particular interest in studying tools aimed at stimulating autonomous reflection on the teaching process, as opposed simply to receiving teaching models.

Computer Mediated Communication

In the twentieth century, the communication revolution has changed, and is continuing to radically transform modern societies by increasing social dislocations and space-time compressions of information transmission. During this period, Computer Mediated Communication (CMC) has deepened this revolution as the technology became not only widespread, but also more sophisticated in the potentialities it provides for creating, collecting, processing and disseminating information. More specifically, and reliant on CMC, in the last decade of the twentieth century, the internet and the World Wide Web (WWW) have created a new type of space in which the communication process takes place. Understanding the impact of CMC and web-based simulations as teaching tools, on the teaching and learning process, depends to a large degree on the theoretical framework one uses to conceptualise the idea of communication itself.

The literature on communication is vast indeed, including no less than four main paradigms cutting across the various disciplines and concerns that attend to the human communication process. In oral societies communicative interaction requires participants to share the same space and time, employing a multiplicity of symbolic cues. By contrast, in print societies, participants may be located in contexts that are spatially and temporally distinct and the symbolic cues available to participants are narrowed and standardised. Moreover, and like electronic media, print is not necessarily oriented towards specific others. The implications for the teaching and learning environments may not be immediately obvious but they are highly significant.

Since the activity of teaching requires effective communication we need to ask what are the structural effects that CMC via the internet, and the WWW impose which differentiates them from traditional print and oral teaching methods. Without understanding the structural conditions imposed by different types of communication media, we cannot appreciate the change brought about by the new technologies or their potential.

From the perspective of the communication environment that these forms of oral and written, i.e., linguistic communicative media, of teaching engender, it is their contrast to the structural conditions imposed by CMC via the internet and the WWW. CMC made its first appearance for pedagogical practice in the arts and social science in the late 1970s and early 1980s mostly as tools for word processing and statistical analysis. By the early 1990s the internet and the WWW began to make inroads into the arts and social science courses as tools for communication and resources. Perhaps the most radical feature of the new communication media is the alterations it makes to the structural conditions of oral, written, and graphical means of communication.

It integrates many of the technologies of communication and information processing developed in the last century into a virtual space shattering many of the structural conditions imposed by the other means of communication. In contrast to traditional lectures, tutorials, seminars, exams, etc., CMC via the internet and the WWW enables both synchronous and asynchronous communication. It means that both unidirectional and bi-directional, as well as multidirectional communication can take place. And it means that both 'events' and 'objects' can be presented simultaneously, though it changes the limitations of both.

In short it means that all pedagogical means of communication can be used simultaneously whilst many of their limitations transcended. Using CMC via the WWW such a lecture can remain a synchronous communication 'event', yet not require presence of participants at the same location. And it also enables an indefinite number of students to attend. Moreover that same 'event', i.,e., can be reproduced on demand as an asynchronous 'event' ie it can become a virtual 'event' that a student can download or trigger online at a different time. The effect is that students rather than lecturers and tutors are placed at the centre of the knowledge acquisition process.

Electronic readers therefore shuttle between two modes of reading, or rather they learn to read in a way that combines verbal and picture reading. Their reading includes activating signs by typing and moving the cursor and then making symbolic sense of the motions that their movements produce. What is clear is that the use of CMC via the internet and WWW requires new skills and competencies to be added to already existing writing and reading skills. Today the core skills, apart from reading and writing, include basic computer familiarity, word processing, telecommunications knowledge including dial-in procedures, online tools including telnet, e-mail and web browser familiarity, online library searches, download routines and ability to use system software for all these functions.

The structural conditions imposed by CMC via the internet and WWW make traditional pedagogical practices more malleable to variations of delivery. Lectures and tutorials that necessitated synchronous presence can now be delivered in both synchronous and asynchronous communication forms. Use of the new communication media also transform the way students, and teachers for that matter, research, read and write. Using hypertext, textual linearity and sequential reading and writing give way to interconnection and collaborative writing.

Moreover, in multivariate environments where outcomes from initial conditions are difficult, if not impossible, to predict with any measure of accuracy, it is often useful to use simulations to evaluate possible outcomes. The idea behind using simulations as pedagogical tools relies on the idea that experience is the best teacher. If access to such experience in real-time is for some reason not possible, then for teaching purposes an artificially created environment may be, if not ideal, at least sufficient. Combined with the fact that the structural conditions of traditional pedagogical communication media have been transformed by the new technologies, it seems reasonable to think that the new multimedia potential of CMC which enable us to create artificial environments for pedagogical purposes, would be used for that purpose more extensively. There are at least three types of simulations currently used for teaching.

The first, and more traditional type of simulation involves CMC only incidentally. The second type of simulation is the computer generated simulation. This type which appears as a software programme, more often on CD-ROM, is really designed for single users, who feed variables into the programme which then uses them to construct an environment appropriate to these variables in the particular field that the programme aims to simulate. The third type, and the one which we will report on here, is the web-based simulation in which CMC is used to create a space in which students playing roles connect to each other and generate the simulation activity in the field being learned. Although a number of web-based simulations have appeared in different disciplines, including nursing, organisational writing, and other courses, the uptake for such simulations has been slow.

The lecturers used to traditional pedagogical practices are reluctant to engage with the new technology for various reasons, including lack of familiarity with the technology, lack of institutional commitment and support, lack of equipment etc. Current thinking on learning and instructional design emphasises precisely the utility of learning activity within context. Viewing learning from this perspective means two things. Firstly, it means that the social, interpersonal and cultural surroundings within which learning occurs affect both the learning process and outcomes. Secondly, 'within context' also means that the skills, strategies, and learning processes are seen as being tightly connected to their immediate contexts of practice rather than as neutral tools available for varied general application.

CMC is a different type of interaction to that supported by videoconference systems, which allow people to be geographically dispersed, but require them to be present at the same time. Computer Managed Learning environments go a step further bringing support for other educational processes into play such as assessment, student tracking and so on.

The main difference between e-mail and a CMC system is that the structure of a discussion is maintained in a coherent model without the user needing to do anything, making it suited to group-based interactions. With e-mail, messages arrive chronologically and are only grouped if the user takes time to put related messages into folders. Even where threading is supported by an e-mail system, discussion threads are often broken if the subject line is changed.

The main thing is not so much the specific system used, but that, given the potentials and limitations of this type of internet application, how lecturers ensure that they use it in a pedagogically effective way. CMC systems allow learners to interact with one another over time. This time independence allows students to fit their online discussions around their other commitments and responsibilities.

Different work patterns can be supported whilst still maintaining a feeling of community amongst the students and staff participating in the course. This is particularly pertinent where students are distributed around the world and potentially in different time-zones.

These systems retain a textual, permanent record of interactions, indicating to a user as they rejoin a discussion which comments have been added since the last time they were there. This is particularly useful if participants have not been able to join in due to, for example, working, other commitments, or illness. It has been found that CMC environments are particularly useful for students for whom English is not their first language. They can take the time to check their understanding without 'missing' any comments as they may do in a face-to-face situation. They can also take their time to compose their replies without being under pressure as in a face-to-face situation.

Learning in a CMC environment can lead to deeper processing of material because time for reflection is allowed. CMC systems provide opportunities for groupwork that would not otherwise exist, e.g., for distance learning students on programmes where all support is done remotely via mail, e-mail or phone/FAX. Where in a more traditional model of support learners may only be able to communicate with their tutor about the subject material and their assignments, use of CMC can allow peer discussion to take place also.

CMC is of course not a panacea. Since it is largely a text-based medium, there is a lack of expressive richness since no non-verbal cues exist to enhance what is being said, and in particular the way that something is being said. Comments can often appear more critical than intended, and great care is needed when this medium is used to give feedback about students' work. The flexibility over time, whilst it has great benefit, can also be a problem for participants. It may be days, depending on the level of activity within a conference, before someone replies to a question.

Decision making can be difficult online, again due to flexibility over time and the notion that everyone can have their say in this environment. Strong chairing is needed to come to a conclusion in an online environment, although some systems support decision making with features such as voting.

Using CMC systems requires access to a computer and the internet, and arguably participants require a certain level of technical competence to overcome any difficulties that arise from accessing the CMC environment. The style of online communication has to be developed by the group.

Different groups develop different norms and styles as they would in a face-to-face situation, but online communication is different in that it is not formal letter writing and neither is it a postcard. Also the level of discourse may be different for different areas of a CMC system.

CMC allows participants to work in ways that may otherwise be impossible due to constraints of time or location. It is difficult to imagine a student body from different continents, collaborating on the design of a web page, for example, in a non-CMC supported distance learning course. Use of CMC allows design discussions and decisions to be made as a group, over time. CMC offers the potential for 'visiting speakers' without the need to have the person physically present.

Online Learning

In many schools, telecommunications resources are becoming more readily available. Student-focused telecommunications programmes and activities are proliferating. But using telecommunications technologies as tools for professional development is a subject still infrequently addressed.

Teachers with in-school access to modems, computers and phone lines may be searching for useful curricular resources, engaging their students in pen-pal relationships with other schools or in multi-site science or social studies investigations, and exchanging e-mail with friends and relatives in distant parts of the globe.

But relatively few teachers are using this technology to participate in structured educational experiences. One possible explanation for the paucity of online professional development opportunities for teachers is that have discovered how to chat, joke, query, and argue online, the kinds of substantive, sustained discussion that is central to learning can still be elusive in online environments. This issue is relevant for student learning as well—particularly as the idea of "virtual schooling" gains momentum.

But most online activities for students are still mediated by teachers, who build on students' online experiences with discussion and elaboration in the classroom. Teachers looking for professional development opportunities are less likely to have someone present to play that role for them.

So the task of providing a structured, rich, and inviting environment for learning within the online experience becomes all the more important. There are a number of practical and pedagogical advantages associated with building virtual learning communities for teachers. On the pragmatic end is the convenience of telecommunications. Since teachers spend the vast majority of their working hours with students in classrooms, there is little time available for professional exchanges with colleagues.

Telecommunications affords teachers the option of communicating with colleagues at times which are convenient to them. The asynchronous nature of communication in this medium means that teachers can establish a rhythm for the exchange of ideas that meshes with the routines of their professional and personal lives. Telecommunications offers an environment in which teachers can reflect on the nature of their professional work.

Composing messages to a community of colleagues gives participants the opportunity to think about their work, to speak about the challenges associated with trying to bring about change in the classroom, and to learn from others who are also sharing their experiences. Perhaps more importantly, experience with telecommu-nications means that the facilitator has had an opportunity to develop an online voice.

When the facilitator offers this kind of established presence on-line, participants gain a clearer impression of who the facilitator is, and learn from her model how to present themselves effectively online. Another important part of the facilitator's role is the choices that they make in how they structure their interactions. This process is influenced by the facilitators' prior experience as classroom teachers; each facilitator draws on techniques they have developed in face-to-face classroom interactions to create their online style.

M-learning

The term, 'mobile learning', means learners are probably more and more mobile, and they use mobile technology. The term 'mLearning' has lately emerged to be associated with the use of mobile technology in education. It seems, however, that it is used in commercial purposes rather than as an educational concept. Although m-learning is a new concept, serving mobile learners is not a new idea. Again, distance education has a history of more than 150 years, where institutions has offered high quality education to learners 'free of time and place'. This means, that if we are willing to accept the concept m-learning, distance teaching institutions have provided m-learning since its invention. Thus, distance education institutions have provided m-learning for many years.

The mobile electronic equipment and communications technologies reintroduce mobility to the distance learner. M-learning is closely related to distance education. The concept, m-learning, from the perspective of educational theory, technology-based definition is obviously not sufficient, and also tries to include aspects of technology. However, it is the challenge of the educational institution to satisfy learning needs for people on the move.

Distance education seems to develop in two quite different directions. The solution at one end of a flexibility continuum can be described as an individual, flexible solution allowing the student freedom to start at any time and follow his own progression according to personal needs for combining studies with work, family and social life, the individual flexible teaching model.

Distance teaching institutions applies normally media and technologies independent of time, such as asynchronous computer communication, video, audio and printed materials. Learning is a change in the student's perception of reality related to the problem areas studied and increased competence in solving problems in a field, ability to differ between focal and more peripheral questions, analytical skills and competence in using the tools within a field in appropriate ways. This means that learning results are shown in a qualitative change in the student's understanding, academic, social and technical competence.

The learning is a result of active processing of learning material and solving problems individually and/or in groups. This view is often different from what we can find in many so-called e-learning programmes, where knowledge often is seen as a larger amount of information or ability to recall and reproduce facts. Learning is an individual process that can be supported by adequate interaction and/or collaboration in groups. Contrary to many other educational providers where the internet is used as a supplement to face-to-face teaching or other forms of distance education, we have followed the philosophy that in principle all communication can be taken care of through the internet, and ideally no obligatory physical meetings should be required.

VIRTUAL-LEARNING OPPORTUNITES AND CHALLENGES

Learners today bring rapidly changing requirements to the learning environment, and the role of universities in our society is changing equally quickly. Virtual universities provide a unique function for today's educational leaders around the world. These cutting-edge universities commonly offer glimpses into the possible future of higher education, while at the same time paving the way for other universities and colleges. The struggles of today's virtual universities will provide the foundation for institutional leaders in the future as they weigh the financial and academic options of distance education.

The primary characteristics of the distance education programmes offered by these unique institutions and those characteristics that may be practical in providing useful educational results through nonconventional educational programs. Distance education has evolved over time from correspondence courses, to educational radio, to educational television, one and two-way teleconferencing, and videoconferencing, to computer assisted/web-based interactive learning opportunities. Yet, with all the technological changes that have evolved in distance education, there have been few changes in the rationale for virtual universities.

The virtual university is intended to offer useful learning opportunities to people at times and locations that are convenient to them. Useful distance education provides a measurable value-added toward achieving the results defined by the ideal vision of a society, the mission objective of an organisation, and the objectives of an individual.

Many educational institutions around the world will offer distance education in the future. Some will use the internet, others will use satellites, and still others will use technologies that one can only dream of today. But those that will make a valuable contribution to learners and society will be those that focus on offering "useful learning opportunities".

During the first half of the nineteenth century, many institutions are offering high-tech distance education, yet few have focused comparable resources on the basic elements of sound instructional and performance system design. These oversights in instructional design have brought most distance education programmes to a point where technology expenditures are exploding, university presidents and boards of trustees are pressing for more effective and efficient institutions, interest from learners in available opportunities is rising, and little progress has been made to validate the value-added of many virtual university initiatives.

Similarly, the variety of delivery media used by virtual universities is equally as extensive as their institutional structures. From text-based courses in the mail to satellite transmissions, delivery of distance education can be structured to meet the requirements of the learner while maintaining a financially feasible model for the institution. Choosing the right delivery system is a decision that should not be made outside of the educational context, however. Depending on the needs of the learners and the desired results of the institution and community, selection of the delivery media may even vary across programmes within a single institution.

There are many educational technologies and institutional structures that can assist in developing successful distance education initiatives. Through dual-mode, as well as single-mode, institutions, learners around the world have more options than ever for achieving laudable objectives through education. Access to these opportunities is, however, only one of the essential components of an educational system focused on the long-term success of learners. Technology of virtual education is still remote from the ordinary experience of most people, it is none the less the dominant means by which human beings are currently remaking the world.

The production, transfer, receipt and representation of data are both the tools and the materials of ordering experience and regulating institutions. The technology so prominent and popular in distance learning is the same technology by which we increasingly conduct manufacturing, commerce, medicine, entertainment, even civic and affectionate association, and war.

Virtual classrooms reflect the escalated commodification of 'real-life' educational practice. The possibilities of the information superhighway touted by the promoters of 'silicon snake oil' have lured many educational institutions to risk educational credibility while exploring the new frontier of cyberspace. The virtual classroom currently operates as an adjunct to conventional distance learning practices and does not reflect or embrace the full potentials available to the virtual organisation. Today, universities and the manner in which students receive their tertiary education is changing.

Sharing information within an educational context, irrespective of the form it takes, fulfils the specific task of fostering a learning environment and a community of scholars. These issues of pedagogy and the consequent learning outcomes are governed by the rituals of discourse. This discourse restricts and structures the fluidity in which specified learning objectives can be achieved. These structures and restrictions impact upon the form and context of educational activity by which information is transmitted and received within the classroom.

This form of information sharing is, however, quite different to those information systems operating at an administrative level. The distinctions that exist for educational practice are more apparent in real-life universities than those which are currently found within the processes of virtual university. These typers of distinction also hallmarks the difference of real-life from a virtual existence. Specific outcomes, beyond the generation of tertiary graduates, must also be accommodated by such universities. Educational imperatives such as excellence in teaching and international research position must continue to be achieved if the guiding rationale of an academic cultural foundation is to continue.

The contemporary practices of universities have dramatically shifted from popular and traditional perceptions of the university. Electronic transmission of text is the new medium being embraced by universities to distribute information to remote, and not-so-remote, students. It contests that regardless of the potential that virtual existence provides for educational practice, if the structured and restrictive organisational practices associated with monolithic and modernist institutions are transposed to this space, the educational potential of the virtual environment will not be realised.

Currently, virutal classrooms currently operate as adjuncts to more conventional distance learning practices. As a result, the educational practices operating in the virtual classroom are an extension of the educational practices of the real-world and do not embrace the full articulation of virtuality that is possible. The traditional and hierarchical organisational structures of universities and the classroom, when contrasted against the dynamic forms of virtual social space and virtual organisations are less fluid and impede the development of educational possibilities in a virtual environment. Institutional virtuality, a particular form of virtual presence, incorporates the compression of time and space as part of its organisational formation.

Virtual space as an interactive medium and educational tool is most suited to those university services and courses that are more transient or more dynamic in nature. This situation is reflected in the types of information that is being adapted to the virtual face of real-life universities, for example, information relating to academics and their current research, as well as existing courses and administrative advice. The application of virtual billboards for the dissemination of information has been relatively successful.

The challenge for educators has been to successfully transform the experience of interactive real-life learning environments into a virtual learning environment. This task has seen total electronic environments such as Multi-user Object Oriented Language (MOOs) and Multi-user Dungeons (MUDs) being adapted as the shell or outer construct of a textually driven classroom.

Virtual universities as they currently exist are amalgams of electronic rooms and electronically warehoused information. These structures however are still restricted by the traditional organisational models of the monolithic tertiary institution.

The traditional and hierarchical structures of the university are reliant upon rules and regulations which stem from older educational practices. For example, the conceptual framework of the lecture, and the lecture theatres themselves remove any doubt as to who will provide the information from which the student will then be expected to learn. These rooms maximise the hierarchical position of the lecturer and reinforces the students, involvement in the machinations of mass education. These relationships construct and reinforce the cultural norms and relationships that hallmark the university and distinguish it from other elements of contemporary society.

The virtual classroom, driven by a lack of corporeality, quickly distorts and challenges these social structures. Virtual universities construct rooms as an environment of exchange for prospective students. These virtual rooms are expected to induce traditional classroom conduct through the cultural associations evoked by a rudimentary simulation of such an environment.

However, it is for this reason that the term virtual university is an oxymoron that cannot represent a serious educational organisational structure. The adaptation of existing real-life information systems does not serve as an adequate model for the fluidity of virtual space. The development of a virtual university is a vastly more complex proposition than the juxtapositioning of the two words. It is a challenge which seeks to translate the solid to the ethereal. Similarly, it is not possible for an organisation operating under modernist frameworks to mimic the structures of commercially orientated virtual organisations. The loose application of extending boundaries through the application of information technology does not automatically predicate a virtual organisation.

Until organisational and departmental formations can accommodate the full potential of cyberspace the virtual university will remain a concept or, at best, an information warehouse, in which inappropriate information systems operate across digital boundaries.

It is important to position virtual space as a phenomenon which is not synonymous with the internet, to appreciate the changes that virtuality imparts upon an information system. Cyberspace is the spatial phenomenon created through the processes of contemporary high technology and is utilised to facilitate human interaction in a manner that is proxy to the capabilities of their bodies. It encompasses the space crafted within video games, the operating theatre of remote surgery, and the virtual lathe of Computer-Aided Manufacturing (CAM). Much of the popular media coverage which equates cyberspace with the internet consequently avoids comparative or inclusive considerations of other spaces.

The popularisation of cyberspace seeks to maximise the useability of the environment and has driven the development of automatic and transparent commercial transactions. Information in this context is understood purely in terms of its consumerability and economic value. The hope, if the internet press can be believed, is to reflect a space in which virtual business is maximised by simulating safe shopping environments that are familiar to consumers in the real-world.

Tensions exist between real-space and virtual space which does not permit the mutual interchange of cultural construction between these spaces. This contradiction encapsulates the problematic possibility of creating a total educational infrastructure in virtual space, where the imperative is to achieve higher learning, yet at the same time provide all the institutional prerequisites that are expected of the university.

The virtual university needs to maintain comparative academic legitimacy in order to provide reassurance to both employers and the institutions of higher education. Information, as an object of desire, and existing information systems must conform to existing protocols to achieve legitimisation. This issue, in itself, is of importance with the development of further tertiary based places which add to an already relatively well catered market. Alternative positions on this situation address the feasibility of these developments and the use of the virtual university as an education medium.

A core component of the university is being altered and this necessitates a re-examination of what defines a university as a university. Changes to the systems through which information is disseminated within universities also holds a bearing upon how learning will be undertaken in these new environments.

In cyberspace, information is transferred from one computer to another through dynamic mechanisms that are formed in the complex amalgam of human agency and software. The transference of knowledge in the form of information atoms is the founding rationale for this space. This spatially dislocated culture of exchange is not a unique phenomenon. The element that differs within these exchanges is the method and medium of communication that are utilised and the form that the exchanged information assumes. Were the form of exchange to be the only significant distinction that was present among these information systems the shift from real to virtual may not represent such a problematic transition.

However, the presence of virtual space is achieved within an environment of compressed of time and space. The social construction of time and space can only exist in relative terms.

Virtual environment and its configuration as a compressed form of time and space is heavily reliant upon the continuous availability of technologically based exchanges. This is an important consideration for defining space as a series of bounded differences.

Being virtual is similarly understood with the association of specific notions of time and space. An object in real life is understood in terms of its associated existence, its connection to reality or its mathematical or scientific representation. A virtual thing has no physical existence, as such, but is made to appear so through software applications. The object in virtual space has no physical or touchable construct although physically can be simulated. The object can be understood to exist in a space that is present through the linking of the computer and telephone.

The existence of virtual spaces challenges existing notions of bound space by blurring the edges of reality. The reality that is constructed through those things which dominate the spaces of daily life can be critically presented as meaning stabilising entities. The existence of objects in cyberspace do not utilise a physical presence for a social meaning to be determined. This dissolution of the solid and physical also presents a challenge to modernist organisational constructs.

The utilisation of MOO's are among recent attempts to overcome the lack of a physical presence within the virtual learning environment. The separation of the individual from the social system reinforces constructs which assert that an ego resides 'within' or somehow inside the individual, whereas, and in distinction, society is somehow positioned outside. In this form of analysis social systems occupy a space outside the individual and are disjointed from a bounded space within the body.

The individual's presence and notion of self are not so easily contained while they are interacting in cyberspace. The participant cannot locate their interactions as solely being conducted at the terminal on which they are working, or at the many hundreds of terminals in which their message might be posted to, or along the electronic cables creating global connectivity. This situation makes notions of place increasingly complex as the decreased need for the association of communication with bodily presence challenges representations of physicality and spatiality. Interactive processes and information exchanges are necessary for the conduct of the business and administration of the university. It is, however, the consumption of material goods and physically bound services that separates the interactivity of organisations located in real-life from those occupying virtual space.

Organisations occupying virtual space differ from real-life organisational structures as all forms of exchange assume a common screen-mediated form that is distinct from a physical item but is still being transacted. A virtual organisation irrespective of its motivating force or projected goal relies upon the reciprocity of mutually shared and traversed space to legitimate a virtual presence. All organisations have an element of virtuality to them. Organisations, as part of their rationale, seek to minimise discrepancies in time and space consensus.

However, in virtual space, operations are conducted in a compressed state in which vast distance and separate aspects of real life spaces are immediately accessible. The associations of time and space formulated according to the scale of weeks, days, hours, minutes and seconds is inappropriate and requires different social constructions of scale and different associations of time to space.

A reassessment of economic worth within the measure of these scales is also needed. These organisational forms are constructed as fluid entities and integrate the knowledge of inevitable and continual change into their structure. The structures and boundaries of these organisations is always at a point of emergence and realignment. The organisation develops as a series of responses to errors and as a counter-manoeuvre to uncertainty. The organisation then establishes within this process maximum stability and consensus.

Maintenance of these boundaries minimises irrationality and unpredictable occurrences within these boundaries. However this process is meant only for those experiencing the social reality found within these boundaries. This positioning problematises the understanding of organisational structure including the university. This view establishes a minimalist perspective and potentially reduces prospects of development.

Modernity and organisations such as universities seek to perfect themselves through the power of rational thought as the claimed essence of humanity. The development of organisations in virtual space and equally the development of virtual organisations in real-space reveal the contradictions found in organisations constructed within a modernist framework.

The virtual organisation is not a fixed entity bound to a physical location or predetermined system. The contradictions of the terms, virtual organisation and virtual university reveals the difficulty in effacing spatial physicality or geographical location from an organisation or bureaucracy which is built around assumptions regarding persistent physicality. The shift to a virtual existence, where information systems are altered due to a virtual presence, is not simply a smooth transition from existing modernist bound rules and regulations.

Information does not have the same protocols that both limit and encompass it in the geographically and physically bound existence of real-life. In colleges and universities, classroom-based activities do support knowledge transfer and acculturation into a discipline or profession—entrance into the guild, so to speak—but the total residential undergraduate experience has another important component: social acculturation, helping young people become civilised, enjoy personal growth, achieve a degree of maturity, and become good citizens.

The post-baccalaureate education and training market is growing rapidly in response to the lifelong learning needs of the emerging knowledge economy and the catalytic boost provided by new, nimble competitors that outsource infrastructure and related instructional technology support in order to create virtual instructional programmes without large investments in bricks and mortar and support staff. In the adult/post baccalaureate market, the 'audience' for educational services changes; it puts a premium on convenience and access.

Virtual learning opportunities are those enabled by the technologies that fall in the space defined by anytime/anyplace. The traditional, brick-and-mortar campuses are really struggling with the extent to which they should offer virtual curricula as opposed to enhancing place/time bound curricula through the use of virtual technologies. For the traditional campus, it is the issue of how to achieve the right bricks-and-mortar balance between bricks-and-mortar programming and opportunities for virtual programming. Virtual service is a service that is delivered dominantly in anyplace/anytime mode. The basic assumption in web terms is that the service receiver, whether an organisation or an individual, has an internet connection and has access to that connection almost any time.

The service provider has no responsibility for providing that access or the PC that attaches to the Net, that is, has no particular facilities responsibility. Virtual technologies really shift the emphasis to the service receivers, who are beginning to demand more convenience and easier access, and technology allows the delivery of these services. Learning has never been just about content. There is too much emphasis placed on content as though every faculty member has built a course from scratch or has written a textbook. In fact, the faculty's role has been about other things: selecting, sequencing and organising the course materials; adding value in the form of guiding self study, giving and grading tests, assigning papers; and, especially, facilitating the shared discovery of knowledge—the classroom as a seminar, not as a lecture.

Many higher educational institutions in the virtual service model are outsourcing their infrastructure and externally obtaining other service functions necessary to deliver their curricula, enabling them to focus on their core intellectual functions. In the long run, it is cheaper, faster to market, and more agile for institutions of higher education to contract for these services rather than to make the capital investments and hire the necessary expertise themselves. E-learning is an opportunity for traditional institutions of higher education to leverage their intellectual capital in new ways. It gives some institutions an opportunity to use their intellectual capital to attract new audiences and even to attract companies willing to make an investment in developing that audience as a for-profit market.

The new virtual-campus constructs, whether created for-profit or non-profit, can give other talented faculty members an opportunity for additional income, sometimes even corporate equity, in an endeavour that can also serve the best interest of their institutions, whether that is in reaching and serving new audiences for a profit or for other reasons related to revenues. A large part of the demand for e-learning does have strong vocational overtones, explicitly the market for virtual adult and post-baccalaureate programmes.

The virtual technologies were typically text-based, locally networked or stand-alone computer-assisted instruction applications. The combination of computation, connectivity, visual and multimedia capacities, and speed have radically changed the potential for technologies in schooling.

Tensions of virtual learning arise because students and teachers now reach out over huge distances to engage each other in learning. The very technology which allows them to connect also swells the tensions always present in education between freedom and control, authenticity and acquiescence. These distances are spatial, temporal, and multitudinously cultural.

Learning in virtual reality makes possible an efficiently abstract relationship between teacher and student. Generically professional teachers dispense and evaluate the learning of generically dutiful students. Individual differences of curiosity, ability or circumstance do not count. Virtual education fulfils several new tendencies in university mass education.

Students usually learn more, and learn more rapidly, in courses that use computer assisted instruction (CAI). Drill and practice is the most common application of CAI in elementary education, the military, and in adult educational settings. In the military, CAI can be more cost-effective than additional tutoring, reduced class size, or increased instruction time to attain equivalent educational gains.

Today, students use multimedia to learn interactively and work on class projects. They use the internet to do research, engage in projects, and to communicate. The new technologies allow students to have more control over their own learning, to think analytically and critically, and to work collaboratively. This "constructivist" approach is one effort at educational reform made easier by technology, and perhaps even driven by it. Traditional lecture methods are often left behind as students collaborate and teachers facilitate. Students, who often know more about technology than the teacher are able to assist the teacher with the lesson.

Since this type of instructional approach, and the technologies involved with it, are recent developments, it is hard to gauge their educational effects. These benefits involve attitudes toward self and toward learning. The studies reveal that students feel more successful in school and are more motivated to learn and have increased self-confidence and self-esteem when using CAI. This is particularly true when the technology allows the students to control their own learning.

In the classroom, the internet and advanced networking technologies are comparative newcomers. Efforts such as Net Day and e-rate discounts enacted by the Telecommunications Act make it easier for many classrooms around the country to connect to the internet. Teachers and administrators use computer and information technologies to improve their roles in the educational process.

REFERENCES

Boud, D. J., "Problem-based learning in perspective", in D. J. Boud, (ed). *Problem-Based Learning in Education for the Professions*, Sydney: Higher Education Research and Development Society of Australasia, 1985.

Cahoon, B., "Teaching and Learning Internet Skills", In *Adult Learning and the Internet*, edited by B. Cahoon, pp. 5-13, *New Directions for Adult and Continuing Education*, no. 78, San Francisco: Jossey-Bass, 1998.

Davie, L. E., and R. Wells, "Empowering the learner through computer-mediated communication", *The American Journal of Distance Education*, 5(1):15-23, 1991.

Gundry, J., "Understanding collaborative learning in networked organisations", In *Collaborative Learning through Computer Conferencing: The Najaden Papers*, ed A. R. Kaye, 167-178, Berlin: Springer-Verlag, 1992.

El-Tigi, M. A, & B. H. Khan, "Web-based learning resources", In B. H. Khan (Ed.), *Web-based training*, Englewood Cliffs, NJ: Educational Technology Publications, 2001.

Engel, C E., "Not Just a Method But a Way of Learning", in Boud D and Feletti, G (eds) *The Challenge of Problem Based Learning*. London: Kogan Page, 1991.

Forsyth, I., *Teaching and Learning Materials and the Internet* (2nd ed.), London: Kogan Page, 1998.

Harasim, L., "Teaching and learning on-line: Issues in computer-mediated graduate courses", *Canadian Journal of Educational Communication*, 16(2):117-135, 1987.

Henri, F., "Distance education and computer-assisted communication", *Prospects* 18(1):85-90, 1988.

Hiltz, S. R., "Evaluating the virtual classroom", In *Online Education: Perspectives on a New Environment*, ed. L. M. Harasim, 133-184. New York: Praeger, 1990.

______________, and Turoff, M., "Structuring computer-mediated communication systems to avoid information overload", Communications of the ACM, 28(7):680-689, 1985.

______________, *The Virtual Classroom: Initial Explorations of Computer-mediated Communication Systems as an Interactive Learning Space*, Newark, NJ: New Jersey Institute of Technology, 1985

Kaye, A., "Computer-mediated communication and distance education", In *Mindweave: Communications, Computers, and Distance Education*, eds. R. Mason and A. Kaye, 3-21, Oxford: Pergamon Press, 1989.

Kearsley G. and B. Shneiderman, "Engagement theory: A framework for technology-based teaching and learning", *Educational Technology*, 38, 5 (September-October 1998), pp. 20-23.

Khan, B. H., "A framework for e-Learning", *e-learning magazine*, December 2001.

Klemm W. R. and J. R. Snell, "Enriching Computer-Mediated Group Learning by Coupling Constructivism with Collaborative Learning", *Journal of Instructional Science and Technology*, 1, No2, 1996.

Phillips, G. M., G. M. Santoro, and S. A. Kuehn, "The use of computer-mediated communication in training students in group problem-solving and decision-making techniques", *The American Journal of Distance Education* 2(1):38-51, 1988.

Rapaport, M., *Computer Mediated Communications: Bulletin Boards, Computer Conferencing, Electronic Mail, and Information Retrieval*, New York: John Wiley & Sons, 1991.

Roberts, L., "A Transformation of Learning: Use of the NII for Education and Lifelong Learning", In D. P. Ely & B. B. Minor (eds.), *Educational Media and Technology Yearbook 1995 / 1996*, pp. 50-66, Englewood, CO: Libraries Unlimited, 1996.

2

Technology in Web-based Learning

The history of the technological revolution reveals that of all the sectors of society, education remains at the bottom of scale when it comes to integrating information technology. The initial slow integration of technology into education can be a derivative of the early visions of distance education. The distance education was first and foremost a movement that sought not so much to challenge or change the structure of higher learning, but to extend the traditional university and to overcome inherent problems of scarcity and exclusivity.

The twenty-first century vision of distance learning has changed as the delivery of education now extends to commercial centres. Along with personal productivity software, windows environments, local area networks, client server computing, internets, intranets, and extranets has come the introduction of personal digital assistants (PDA), and mobile and wireless technologies.

These technological advances have enabled electronic commerce systems, anytime, anyplace data retrieval and updating, education, professional development, and the rapid growth of e-learning. As the integration of technology and education becomes addressed and as innovative information technology continues to surprise us, it is critical that a systemic approach to the organisational process and individual issues such as insufficient empirical research, minimal application of research to practice, and application of traditional instructional design and teaching methods need to be addressed. In addition, the ineffective use of technology, the absence of the learner in the instructional design, antiquated policy; intellectual property and inadequate online teacher training are other issues affecting the effective integration of technology and education.

E-learning sometimes referred to as online learning, web-based learning, distance learning and technology-based learning, among other names, is a concept that has garnered significant global attention. With e-learning being a huge imperative for government, business, and professional associations, and with these institutions being major players in the advancement of e-learning, it is important to be cognizant of and synthesise what these institutions purport about e-learning.

If government, business, and professional associations are leading the advancement of e-learning, it is critical that there be cognizance on what these institutions say about the purpose, features and trends of e-learning. This basic information can be the foundation to focusing research on e-learning, a focus that is direly needed. E-learning is the acquisition and use of knowledge distributed and facilitated primarily by electronic means. This form of learning currently depends on networks and computers but will likely evolve into systems consisting of a variety of channels (e.g., wireless, satellite), and technologies (e.g., cellular phones, PDA's) as they are developed and adopted.

The integration of education and technology, though presently lagging behind other aspects of society, will get better as technology improves and leaders in private and public institutions create partnerships to integrate technology into their education programmes to improve learning and performance.

Learning and performance are outcomes of e-learning that hold promise given the features of e-learning. The learner will have control of the learning; a model that has been found to be the best in an online environment. The just-in-time, anywhere, anytime capabilities will be topped off by the opportunities for collaboration, interactivity and personalisation. Therefore, as business organisations discuss the growing markets of e-learning and develop business models to attract investors, the government targets policy makers, educators, employers and the public at large, while professional organisations mainly focus on the workforce and workplace, it is imperative that all three entities become aware of their convergences and divergences. While there is a growing recognition of and attention to distance learning in higher education, its growing inclusion in academia significantly changes the educational environment and experience.

EVOLUTION OF LEARNING TECHNOLOGIES

Most recently, CD-ROMs were the delivery medium of choice, but even before that distance learning was accomplished through the use of video and audiotapes in learning experiences when being there in person wasnot an option, although the absolute costs of these latter technologies may be low in comparison to the networked technologies being introduced today.

Computer-based training (CBT) relies mainly on CD-ROM. One of the main benefits of CBT is that it does not face the bandwidth problems that web-based training (WBT) does. Due to its large storage capacity, a CD-ROM can deliver rich multimedia presentations without clogging up a network by downloading large audio or video files. Many would even argue that the presentation of content has taken a step backward as it has migrated from CD-ROM to the internet because of the relative lack of multimedia components.

The downside of training on a CD-ROM, though, is its static nature. Once produced and distributed the content on the CD-ROM cannot be changed no matter how fast it becomes outdated. Organisations that utilise CD-ROMs for training soon find that they have invested in a library of titles that quickly reach the point of obsolescence.

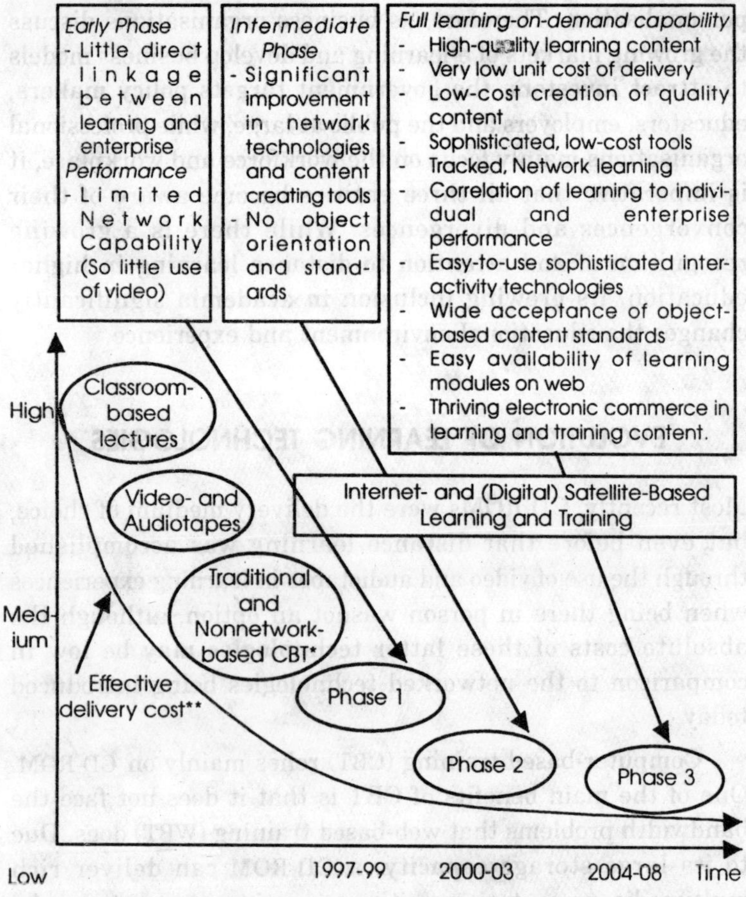

Figure 2.1: Evolution of Technology-based Learning

*CBT = computer-based training

** The cost curve assumes the following:

- A networked-based approach significantly reduces the need for classroom-based sessions and thus eliminates many learners' travel and lodging costs.
- The company already had made investments in intranets and websites. Thus, marginal investments in network-based learning are for the preparation of learning modules.
- The network-based approach is a highly effective learning mode.
- Actual costs relate to learning effectiveness.

Source: SRI Consulting

Distance education offerings sprouted up on the web, sometimes offered by accredited academic institutions or reputable training providers, but more often as the products of no-name providers. While some of the unbranded contents was no doubt of high quality, the programmes that were had a bad taste in the mouths of consumers and educators alike.

Today, web collaboration tools are ready for prime time, and learning management systems (LMS) have been developed that can track, manage, and tie together an entire enterprise-wide programme of learning. A number of vendors have begun to bundle all of these tools together into one package to create integrated learning systems that can either be hosted by the customer or the vendor to address organisational learning needs. The following are some of the major developments in e-learning:

i) Highly relevant content will be easy to find, purchase, and deliver through an organisation's learning platform.
ii) More sophiscated content management tools will be able to create highly customised courses on the fly for learners, using reusable learning object technology.
iii) Learning management systems will monitor and adjust an individual's learning programme, taking into account the learner's existing proficiencies, job role, learning objectives, learning style, and preferred delivery method. The LMS will also be able to carefully track and analyse a user's progress in programmes of learning over long periods of time.
iv) Training will be linked to performance on both an individual and organisation-wide level, so that the return on the investment in learning can be more accurately measured.

These developments are already becoming reality and we expect the rest to follow in short order. But these capabilities, for the most part, represent the value-added surrounds of e-learning—

that is, the features that make e-learning a valuable organisational asset from the point of view of an administrator or corporate trainer. They don't actually address the value to the learner. Therefore, let us now take a look at how an end-user might actually experience e-learning. Learning management system will play an important role in the facilitation of a learning object strategy. The management system will serve as a type of gateway where content enters, is assembled into meaningful lessons based on the learner's profile, and is presented to the learner, whose progress is then tracked by the management system. It is crucial, therefore, that the system be able to operate with content and tools from multiple sources.

Today through the emergence and development of networked technologies, learners can participate in a variety of different learning experiences, at least one of which is likely to meet anyone's requirements for topic schedule, and format.

Synchronous Shared Learning (SSL) could probably be most closely compared with a traditional classroom learning experience. The learners and instructor are all logged on to a live, web-based collaborative learning environment and are participating in the class at the same time. This format allows the students to ask questions and receive answers, contribute to a discussion, or ask the professor to alter the pace of the class—all in real-time. The benefit of SSL is that any group of people with a keen interest in a certain subject can have a shared learning experience, without geography being an obstacle. While SSL format maintains the shared learning aspects that many see as the primay benefit of traditional instruction, it does not address the issue of scheduling. One of the main reasons that a learner may opt for an online course is because of time constraints associated with work or family obligations.

The independent e-learning (IEL) format can also be more of a "just-in-tune" experience; in other words, the learner does not have to operate on the timeframe dictated by the course provider, as she would in a shared learning experience. One of the most important features of the LMS will be its ability to conduct pre-assessments so that relevant courses can be built from modular learning object.

The current e-learning technologies are exciting and today's applications are only scratching the surface of what is possible. The richness of an e-learning experience is most severely limited by bandwidth constraints. The use of multimedia components such as audio, video, animations are only feasible if the learner has ample width to receive them. However, the ability to include multimedia components is often what makes e-learning options attractive in the first place.

TECHNOLOGICAL INFRASTRUCTURES

Computers and internet technologies can improve teaching and learning, strengthen teacher professional development, support broad educational reform, enhance school-community partnerships, and improve school management. The demand to realise these educational objectives by integrating computer and internet technologies into education forces education planners, principals, teachers, and technology specialists to make many decisions about the technical, training, financial, pedagogical, and infrastructure requirements of school computerisation programmes.

There is no single best computer configuration or single infrastructure solution to suit all situations. Rather, there are only optimum solutions for each school. Arriving at these optimum solutions is not simply a technical process but requires a careful consideration of educational goals and an understanding of the different costs and benefits, both economic and educational, of different technology options. Since infrastructural questions are dominated by a complex mix of technical factors, requirements, and options, decisions about infrastructure often are divorced from educational concerns and driven by technical matters and technology experts.

In reality, infrastructure questions and decisions are coupled with educational needs, opportunities, and outcomes. Therefore, to achieve optimum educational results, each school or school system should base infrastructure decisions on an assessment of a mix of technical factors and educational needs and objectives. The results of such an assessment then must be compared to the costs and benefits of a variety of computer system configurations and infrastructure options.

Enhancing teacher professional development by training teachers both to use computer and internet technologies and to integrate these technologies into education, along with improving subject matter competence and strengthening pedagogical skills, are often important objectives of school computer programmes.

Ensuring that such objectives are achieved often requires that teachers be provided with special access to computer and internet technologies and a complex mix of initial and ongoing training and support. If online professional development is planned, suitable internet connectivity and time to engage in online learning will be required.

Most schools calculate this ratio by simply dividing the number of students in the school by the number of computers available to students. In secondary schools, the issue is viewed more appropriately in terms of how much computer and internet access, frequency, and duration students in different disciplines have. One of the major questions about school computer systems focuses on whether to install computers in classrooms or computer labs. If classrooms are small and crowded and without lockable doors, it may be more appropriate to use labs. Creating optimum lighting conditions, especially where electrical light may be difficult to manage, often can be achieved most easily by modifying computer labs for skylights rather than trying to adjust the lighting in every room in a school.

The simplest way to connect computers to the internet is through telephone lines and a dial-up connection to an internet service provider (ISP). However without existing phone lines, it can prove difficult and expensive to provide wiring for telephone connections in more than just one or two computer labs. Providing sufficient security in the classroom and at the school to prevent theft of equipment, software, and supplies can be expensive and it is often only possible for one or two rooms in a school. When security plans are made, it is important to achieve a balance between protecting equipment from theft and allowing easy access to computers as often as possible. Fears of being blamed for damage to or loss of equipment can cause principals and teachers to make it very difficult for students to use computers, or for community members to benefit from investments in technology through after-school use.

Schools with large numbers of students per classroom are likely to have limited space for permanently installed computers. Under such conditions, it may be best to install computers in one or more lab facilities where students can use the equipment. For smaller children, it is possible to have two to four students per computer. However, it is difficult and restrictive to have more than two older students per computer. To allow multiple students per computer requires sufficient space between computers with enough room left over to allow teachers to move among students to review work and offer support and feedback.

The high cost of investing in technology in public schools often can be justified partly by allowing the new computer facilities to be used by members of the school community. If this is a priority, then a lab or computers-on-wheels configuration may be needed, necessitating additional investments in staff and security. Computers operate better and last longer when the electricity that powers them is continuous and of consistent voltage.

Many schools, especially older ones, have an insufficient supply of electricity to withstand the additional demand made by the computers. Further, electrical cables may not be the correct gauge to withstand the additional load caused by computers being connected to the school's electrical system. Or the electrical cables may be composed of aluminum, which oxidizes over time and can become a fire hazard. Lack of electricity or poor wiring may require the school to refurbish the existing electrical system or add a whole new electrical supply system. This is one reason why many schools decide to install computers in labs, which reduces the amount of electrical wiring needed.

Also, computers, especially those connected to a local area network (LAN), require a grounded electrical system to operate smoothly and trouble-free. Again, this is less costly if done to one or two computer labs or rooms, rather than to the entire school. The quality of electricity coming to a school also may be inconsistent and fluctuate between low and high voltages. These conditions can disrupt students' use of computers and result in premature and sudden failure of expensive computer equipment.

These problems are often dealt with by installing line stabilisers to make the voltage constant and uninterruptible power supplies to provide a short-term supply of electricity to the computer to allow work to be saved and equipment to be turned off safely when the electrical supply fails. Adding this equipment to a school computerisation plan can increase costs significantly. When electricity is not available, it may be possible to install solar-powered systems for the computer equipment.

Solar equipment can be very expensive and is often best used with laptop computers, since they use less power and can use direct current (DC) electricity directly. Also, since laptops come with their own batteries, less money may need to be spent on a battery back-up system for the solar panels.

Learning-disabled students may need special keyboards with large keys and audio and tactile feedback to engage the technology effectively. Computer technologies have had some of their greatest impact in educating special-needs students. However, ignoring their special mobility and technological needs at the start of the planning and design process will guarantee that these benefits will be unrealised.

Modern computers and cathode ray tube monitors generate a great deal of heat. The lack of sufficient ventilation, especially in humid climates, can result in a very uncomfortable working environment for students and, occasionally, can even cause computers to overheat and malfunction. However, opening windows to improve air circulation can result in a damaging level of dust entering the computer room and increased risk of equipment theft.

The combination of heat and dust often forces school computer programmes to install expensive air conditioning units. Before committing to the purchase of air conditioning systems, programmes should consult with architects, often as volunteers, about alternative strategies suitable for local environments to keep computer labs comfortable and free of excessive dust.

Connecting computers together in a LAN can have significant educational benefits. At the same time, creating a LAN has financial and infrastructure effects that need to be weighed carefully against possible educational gains. LANs, if carefully planned, can be installed after the initial computer system is put in place if funding prohibits installation at the start. However, careful planning will be needed to avoid any duplication of effort and wasted investment.

Technology budgets for initial installation of systems and ongoing support likely will be a decisive factor when deciding which configuration is best for a school or school system. As a result, budgets for ongoing equipment support, supply, repair, and replacement often are neglected or insufficient. Also, funds to purchase and install equipment and provide initial teacher training may come from national or state budgets.

In contrast, local government and school budgets often will have to cover the purchase of consumables, pay for connectivity, and fund technical support and maintenance to keep the systems running. Without additional funds, these ongoing responsibilities and recurrent expenses often are not met. It may be necessary, therefore, for schools to devise special fund-raising schemes such as opening up the computer system to fee-based use during nonschool hours, reaching out to parent-teacher associations (PTAs), and soliciting the local business community for funding. In addition, where families have sufficient disposable income, some schools have charged an annual computer use fee to cover the cost of consumables and equipment maintenance. No matter what the solution, schools should develop and implement strategies immediately to guarantee sustainability of their computer systems.

The technology will not enable teachers to use computer and internet technologies to enhance learning significantly. Initial and ongoing teacher professional development focusing on using computers and effective pedagogy usually is required to enable schools to gain the greatest educational benefit from their investments in computers.

The configuration of computer facilities plays a major role in providing effective learning opportunities and professional development for teachers. Achieving the multiple benefits of classroom-based computers demands significant financial investments to:

i) purchase sufficient hardware and software so that all classes have equal access to computers;
ii) refurbish all classrooms so that there is sufficient room for the computers and a suitable electrical supply, security, networkability, and connectivity;
iii) provide each teacher with a high degree of computer technical and pedagogical skills since education technology specialists will not be available to help as they would in a computer lab; and
iv) supply ongoing technical and educational support.

Some schools may decide to install only one or two computers per classroom, which likely will have little or no impact on learning. Experience also shows that when there is only a single computer in a classroom, it often becomes the "teacher's" computer and is rarely used by students.

Considerations for installing computers in classrooms include:

a) *Teachers' skills*: Computers in classrooms usually require teachers to have a high degree of technical skill and the capacity to integrate computer use into their teaching.
b) *Space and student numbers*: Placing clusters of computers in a classroom to enable effective student use requires enough space for both the computer systems and groups of two to three students to sit comfortably in front of the computers, circulation area for teachers and non-traditional student seating arrangements.
c) *Quality and availability of electricity*: Computers demand a quality electrical supply.
d) *Security*: Maintaining sufficient security to prevent theft of equipment, software, and supplies, while also enabling open access to the classrooms to a variety of users, is usually impossible.
e) *Availability of maintenance and support services*: Distributing computers throughout the classrooms in a school makes it more difficult, and more expensive, to provide effective maintenance and support services dealt with at the very start of devising a school computer plan.

There are many ways to describe different infrastructure needs and computer system configuration options and strategies. There are four organising themes:

i) physical configuration options,
ii) networking technology options,
iii) internet access options, and
iv) software and operating system considerations.

Computers can be distributed in schools in three basic ways to meet educational goals. They can be provided to individual classrooms; installed in central computer labs, libraries, and teachers' planning rooms; or moved from room to room on mobile carts. Each of these options, and combinations of them, has associated benefits and costs that need to be considered carefully to select the options that best meet a school's needs.

These are overly simplistic perspectives because the distribution of computers is only one factor in determining how teachers and students use them, and the internet, to enhance teaching and learning.

The potential benefits of distributing computers to individual classrooms is to provide teachers and students with easier access to these educational tools. More specifically, having computers in classrooms can:

i) make it easier for teachers to integrate computer and internet use into routine educational programmes—but

ii) this cannot be guaranteed;

iii) allow for spontaneous use of these tools during instructional activities;

iv) provide even limited internet access in each classroom via intermittent use of a single dial-up phone connection, and this can be expensive, and high-speed access can become prohibitive.

Connecting computers within the classroom and the school: Most schools require extensive remodelling to enable computers in classrooms and schools to be connected to form cabled networks. Also, creating classroom networks can require significant investments in additional hardware.

Community access to school-based computer systems: Installing computers in classrooms can make it more difficult to provide community access to these costly resources. This difficulty is exacerbated if the number of computers per classroom is relatively low, since no single room may have a sufficient number of computers to meet community use and training needs.

As a result, schools with classroom-based computers may not be able to generate enough revenue to cover the costs of consumables, maintenance, and replacement of systems through community access to their computers. With sufficient funding, and under the right conditions, with highly skilled teachers, classroom-based computers can have a significant impact on the quality of teaching and learning.

Classroom-based computer installations with low student-to-computer ratios also can provide unparalleled student access to computer use and enable teachers to integrate the use of computers and the internet in ways that cannot be achieved by any other configuration. However, for most schools, especially those in developing countries and poor communities, it is not possible to install computers routinely in classrooms. Under these more common conditions, alternative strategies must be considered.

Some software titles are no longer published and are primitive by today's standards, with black and white graphics, no sound other than beeps and chirps, and no wildly interactive screens. An integrated use of computers in classroom makes learning more effective and fun for her and for the students. It also makes it possible to individualise instruction at a level not possible without computers and allows to meet the learning needs of each student. It also enables planned and spontaneous peer-to-peer instruction among students.

Mixing computer use with routine classroom activities allows for complex student-organised and -managed, project-based, and collaborative learning activities that often extend beyond curriculum themes.

A major goal of cooperative learning is to help students expand their repertoire of problem-solving approaches, and the second goal is to help them develop collaborative skills—leadership, decisionmaking, communication, etc. These goals can only be achieved if students have enough time to develop a group dynamic, encountering and overcoming difficulties in working together.

The only way cooperative learning will work is if students are given every incentive to help one another. If students are guaranteed a given grade and if they meet a specified standard, they have everything to gain and nothing to lose by cooperating; if they know that by helping someone else they could be hurting themselves (as is the case when grades are curved), cooperation is finished.

Computer Labs in Schools

Computer labs are popular way to provide equitable access to computers for the greatest number of users at the lowest possible cost. Computer labs enable schools to concentrate expensive resources in a common space that can be used for student educational activities, teacher professional development events, and community groups. When using computer labs, it is important to arrange computers along the walls of the room rather than in rows facing the front of the room, so teachers can view all the students' work from a common point and move quickly and easily from student to student, providing feedback, support, and guidance.

This arrangement also can make it easier and less costly to provide electricity and network access for the computers. Establishing computers in a lab or dedicated room only requires schools to install quality electricity, network cabling and servers, internet access, effective security, climate control systems, good lighting, and specialised furniture in one or two rooms in a school rather than in many different rooms.

Computer labs can be maintained by one or two staff members who also can provide technical and pedagogical support to teachers. Equipment and software can cost less for computer labs used by all classes than for classroom-based systems.

Computer labs can optimise return on technology investments if their use is scheduled effectively. It can be easier and less costly to provide access to the internet via computer labs than with classroom systems since many computers can use a common connection to the internet.

Computer labs can make it easier to encourage collaborative interdisciplinary projects among groups of teachers and students. Computer labs make it easier to provide community access to computer systems for public relations, and to generate revenue to cover the costs of consumables, internet connectivity, and replacement of old equipment. They can become oversubscribed quickly, and competition for use may make it difficult for teachers to engage their students in longer-term projects and activities.

Scheduling conflicts can frustrate teachers and inhibit their use of computer labs. In some schools, principals or lab coordinators may implement policies designed to keep the computers safe at the expense of using them. Schools can overcome many of the challenges of using school computer labs by devising and implementing effective policies governing the use of the labs. A computer lab coordinator is a critical asset and can continue to promote use of the lab and help teachers deal with scheduling conflicts.

Computers-on-Wheels (or COWs) systems are essentially rolling carts that hold one or more computers, usually laptops, often with a printer, and with the possibility to connect the cart to the school LAN via a single classroom network connection. COWs can be brought into a classroom, often by an educational technology specialist, when the teacher wants to use computers for a specific activity. The following are the some of the benefits and challenges of using COWs:

i) COWs make it possible to provide teachers access to computers in their classroom without having to remodel the room significantly, provide special furniture, or reserve space for dedicated computers Working in small groups at their desks enables all students to have access to computers even in crowded classrooms. Using battery-powered laptops makes it possible to avoid providing special electrical power or installing additional power outlets.

ii) Using infrared printing and wireless networking cards enables the students to print their work and connect to each other and the school network for e-mail, electronic communication, and, possibly, internet access without cables.

iii) COWs allow schools to optimise the use of expensive equipment by enabling teachers to request a cart of computers.

iv) COWs may be more affordable than remodelling classrooms, building special computer labs, providing special electrical supplies, installing cabling to network all the computers, and buying special furniture. Since software only needs to be purchased for the computers on the carts, and not for dozens of computers in each classroom, the cost of software can be much less with COWs than with classroom-based installations.

v) COWs can be stored in secure rooms when not in use.

vi) COWs can provide access to computers in situations where students have classes in different rooms. COWs can be customised to include expensive specialised equipment that normally would not be part of a classroom system.

vii) COWs often are brought to classrooms by an educational technology specialist who can help teachers to make effective use of the computers in teaching and provide immediate technical support.

viii) COWs can be used in teacher professional development programmes. COWs can be used to support school-community computer programmes because they can be brought to the room in the school used by community members.

ix) The cost per computer to create a COW system with laptops and wireless networking capabilities is higher than for conventional desktop computer systems.

x) There is a greater risk of equipment damage from accidents, hard use, or dropping. Dedicated staff is often needed to maintain COW systems, deliver them to teachers, and help teachers set up and use the equipment.

xi) Schools with multiple floors and no elevators have to have COWs for every floor or restrict their use to specific floors.

xii) COWs can perpetuate the belief that computers in education should be limited to "special" computer-aided activities. COWs, especially when used in secondary schools, can limit opportunities for interdisciplinary teaching and learning, since it can be more difficult to bring a mix of teachers and students together in a one-teacher classroom than in a common space.

For schools with few extra rooms for labs and no space or funds to build them, COWs offer a cost-effective way to provide teachers and students with access to computers and internet connectivity. If COWs are used, effort should be made to promote the use of the COWs and to help teachers move beyond simple uses of computers in education. Without added educational inputs, COW systems can fall into disuse and rarely find their way into the classroom.

Computer labs then can be used for whole class access and interdisciplinary use. Library computers can be used to focus on research activities, while special classrooms can be outfitted with computers, especially for special-needs students, creating benefits that are difficult to achieve from computer labs. The combination of these different options with one or more computer labs can create an ideal solution to providing students and teachers with access to these rich and powerful educational tools. Connecting computers together to form a network, and connecting school, lab, and classroom networks to the internet can multiply the educational value and impact of computers in schools.

There are a variety of options for creating classrooms, lab, and school computer LANs:

i) *Peer-to-peer networking*: As with all networked computers, users can share files and resources located on computers in the network. With peer-to-peer networking, however, there is no file server or central computer to manage network activity. One or more of the computers in a peer-to-peer network can provide centralised services such as printing and access to the internet. Most desktop operating systems come with software to enable peer-to-peer networking once the computers are connected by some cable or wireless networking infrastructure. Peer-to-peer networking is good for small networks where a centralised file server is not needed and network security is not a major issue. This type of networking is less expensive to set up since the only additional expense is in the cables and networking hardware.

ii) *Client / Server Networking*: As a computer network grows in size and complexity, it may be necessary to shift to a client/server style of network using more advanced network operating software. One of the advantages of client/server networks is that they are scalable: more clients and servers can be added to the system without changing the network significantly. These centralised networks are easier to manage, administer, and secure than peer-to-peer networks. These benefits come with some disadvantages, however. Due to the need to have a central "dedicated" server, initial costs are higher. Also, they are more complex to set up and maintain than stand-alone computers and peer-to-peer networks, often requiring schools to hire a technician to oversee the network.

In contrast, thin clients are desktop appliances or network devices that link the keyboard, monitor, and mouse to a server where all applications and data are stored, maintained, and processed. The server, often called an application server, is built to provide all networking services and computer calculations.

Since all network and computer services are centralised, all maintenance and upgrading is done at the server; there is no need to service the clients. Proponents of thin-client/server networks emphasise that even though initial purchase costs are usually higher than with traditional PC/server networks, lifetime costs or total cost of ownership can be significantly less.

Thin-client/server networks are also easier to install than traditional client/server networks. In addition, since the client appliances cannot function without the server, there is little risk of theft. Thin-client systems are very efficient at providing access to the internet, and, because the client appliances have few moving parts and limited functions, thin-client/server networks are more reliable and stable than traditional network systems.

A major disadvantage of some thin-client/server networks is that little educational software is written to run on thin-client servers running a version of UNIX. Most of these servers come with special emulation software, but this is usually an incomplete solution: software often runs slower and some applications fail to function. Since many thin-client/ server networks are based on a type of UNIX operating system, skills with UNIX are needed to set up and administer. However, if schools have no staff with these skills, but do have access to the internet, it is possible to have a technician at some remote site administer and maintain the network.

Wireless LANs

This type of system does not require cables to connect computers to each other and to the server and shared peripherals. Instead, wireless network adapters (receivers) are installed in all computers that will be part of the network. One or more wireless network hubs/transmitters are connected to the server, usually by a cable. Network traffic is then transmitted by the hub to each computer and to and from the server.

Wireless LANs have many advantages:

i) They can be installed and configured in a very short time, since limited or no construction is needed.
ii) They allow for a high degree of flexibility. Computers, especially laptops, can be moved around a room or building, within the range of the network signal, without losing their connection to the LAN.
iii) They can be less costly to install and use than conventional cabled systems.
iv) They allow schools to create customised LAN systems covering single rooms or whole sections of the school.
v) They also can be mixed with cabled systems to create greater flexibility.

Wireless LANs are not a perfect solution for all environments. The speed of network traffic depends on how many computers are using the hub's bandwidth simultaneously the distance from the hub and the thickness and character of walls between the transmitter and receiver can affect the speed and quality of the network signal significantly. Due to the benefits of wireless LANs and their growing popularity, the technology is improving rapidly, and new standards with higher transmission rates are emerging. Over the next few years, the speed and range of transmission will increase, and reliability and security will improve. Wireless LANs will become an increasingly desirable LAN solution for school computer systems.

Power Line LANs (PLN)

Power line networking (PLN) currently is capable of providing reliable network communication speeds between 250 Kbps and 500 Kbps for six to 20 network access points. Equipment costs are higher than conventional and wireless networking technologies, but these are expected to fall as technical improvements are made and larger-scale systems become available. By accessing the internet, computers can become powerful communication devices with many educational applications. A variety of options and technologies should be considered when deciding whether and how to access the internet. If direct connection to the internet is not possible, for economic or technical reasons, students and teachers can still gain simulated access to a selection of internet resources by copying valuable websites to CD-ROMs. Then they can use the CDs to access these sites, thus simulating the internet.

The CDs, which are updated periodically, use the same browsers that are used with the internet, so that when internet access becomes available, teachers and students will have no difficulty using this technology. Internet access to a single computer (for example, in a lab, classroom, teachers' room, or library) or, by using software on a server, networked computers can share this single connection.

Schools can get faster and more reliable internet access by using permanent "dedicated" high-speed connections where they are available and affordable. A variety of dedicated high-bandwidth options may be available to schools, including integrated services digital network (ISDN), digital subscriber line (DSL), terrestrial wireless, digital cable, radio modem, and satellite access. Several new technologies offer the potential for developing countries to leapfrog earlier generations of equipment to provide connectivity.

Terrestrial wireless and satellite technologies offer many advantages because they do not require installation of wireline networks. Satellite facilities also can be installed where communication is needed, even in remote and isolated areas, rather than waiting for terrestrial networks to be extended from the cities.

Cellular telephony has become the first and only telephone service for many people in developing countries, where it may be available much sooner than fixed-line service. In countries such as Cote d'Ivoire, Gabon, Rwanda, Tanzania, Uganda, Cambodia, and the Philippines, there are now more cellular telephones than fixed lines.

For example, the community tele-centre in Buwama, Uganda, about 60 km from Kampala, connects to the internet via cellular modem. However, cellular access is often quite costly, and bandwidth is limited. It is likely to be more practical for short bursts of use for e-mail communication than for surfing the web.

Wireless local loop systems can be used to extend local telephone services to rural schools without laying cable or stringing copper wire. Thus, instead of a fixed-line connection, schools would have a wireless link to the telecommunications network. Wireless local loop costs have decreased, making it competitive with copper.

Wireless systems enable faster extension to new users than extending wire or cable; they also have a lower ratio of fixed to incremental costs than copper, making it easy to add more customers and serve transient populations. Wireless is also less vulnerable than copper wire or cable to accidental damage or vandalism. Countries with wireless local loop projects include Bolivia, Czech Republic, Hungary, Indonesia, South Africa, and Sri Lanka. If the telephone company does not provide wireless local loop, schools may be able to install or lease their own wireless links to the internet. Point-to-point fixed wireless, such as microwave systems, can provide high-speed internet access by connecting to an ISP's point of presence (POP).

Short-range cordless extensions can provide the link from wireless outstations to subscriber premises; the DECT (digital European cordless telephone) technology standard also can allow the base station to act as a wireless private branch exchange (PBX) and reduce costs further.

The wireless protocol has been developed to make it possible to transmit web pages and other data to cellular phones. It can be adapted for wireless services in developing countries so that internet information can be transmitted to low-bandwidth wireless systems. However, the variety of web content accessible through devices enabled by this protocol is still very limited.

Third-generation mobile networks are beginning to be introduced in some industrialised countries, and eventually may be made widely available in developing regions. They offer greatly increased bandwidth over existing mobile networks, with the possibility of internet access to hand-held devices such as portable phones, personal digital assistants, and small personal computers. However, the capital cost of upgrading existing networks is very high, and the price of access for internet applications may be greater than for other options.

Satellite Technologies

Very small aperture terminals (VSATS): Small satellite earth stations operating with geosynchronous satellites can be used for interactive voice and data as well as for broadcast and reception. For example, banks in remote areas of Brazil are linked via VSATs, and the National Stock Exchange in India links brokers with rooftop VSATs. VSATs for television reception deliver broadcasting signals to viewers in many developing regions, particularly in Asia and Latin America.

Internet gateways can be accessed via geostationary satellites. Also, there is a half-second delay in transmission via geosynchronous satellites, although it is a more obvious hindrance for voice than data. Upstream connectivity is provided over existing phone lines. This approach is designed for rural areas with telephone service, but where bandwidth is very limited.

Interactive access via VSAT: Several companies offer fully interactive internet access via satellite; examples include Gilat, Hughes Gateway, and Tachyon. Systems typically are designed for small-business or home office use, but could be a solution for schools with no other communication options. Geosynchronous satellites designed for interactive voice and data can be used for data broadcasting as well. For example, the WorldSpace satellite system delivers digital audio directly to small radios. It can also be used to deliver internet content; schools or telecentres can identify which websites they want to view regularly, and WorldSpace broadcasts the data for reception via an addressable modem attached to the radio.

Global mobile personal communications systems: Using low earth-orbiting satellites, these systems provide voice and low-speed data virtually anywhere, using hand-held transceivers. However, the price per minute for these services is typically much higher than national terrestrial services, and the first generation of low earth-orbiting satellites has very limited bandwidth.

Store-and-forward messaging: Volunteers in Technical Assistance (VITA) has developed a satellite-based system called VITAsat, capable of delivering sustainable, low-cost communications and information services to remote communities. The system uses simple, reliable, store-and-forward e-mail messages relayed to the internet via low earth-orbiting satellites. Using compression technology and software that allows access to web pages using e-mail, VITAsat can make the internet accessible virtually anywhere. VITA plans to include local skill and organisational capacity building and development of targeted information content and services designed specifically to meet the needs of small businesses, local NGOs, educators, health workers, and other relief and development workers. Constellations of low earth-orbiting satellites such as Teledesic and new generations of geosynchronous satellites such as Loral's Cyberstar and Hughes's Spaceway will be designed to offer bandwidth on demand for internet access, videoconferencing, and distance education.

Wireline Technologies

Innovations in wireline technology make it possible to provide high-speed internet access over telephone lines, rather than having to upgrade existing copper networks. These technologies may be used in urban areas where basic telephone service is available.

Integrated services digital network (ISDN): Regular twisted-pair copper telephone lines can carry two 64 kbps channels plus one 16 kbps signalling channel. One channel can be used for voice and one for fax or internet access, or two can be combined for videoconferencing or higher-speed internet access. Developed in Europe, ISDN may be available from telephone companies in some urban and suburban areas of developing countries.

Digital subscriber line (DSL): Several variations of DSL technology have been developed that provide data rates from 384 kbps or more downstream over existing telephone lines. This technology is replacing ISDN in industrialised countries because of its greater bandwidth. It can be used in urban areas where copper wire is already installed, but its range is limited to about 1 km from a telephone exchange.

Like DSL, cable offers much higher bandwidth than dial-up telephone lines. However, a high volume of users may result in congestion of a shared cable network, and older networks may not be converted easily for two-way connectivity. Telephone companies upgrading their networks may install optical fibre for institutional customers such as hospitals, schools, and businesses. The advantage of fibre is its enormous bandwidth, which can be used for high-speed internet accessing or other services such as videoconferencing. However, the price of access may be prohibitive. Some schools have managed to gain free or heavily discounted access to so-called "dark fibre", excess capacity that has been installed but is not yet in use.

Hybrid fibre/coax: A combination of optical fibre and coaxial cable can provide broadband services such as TV and high-speed internet access as well as telephony; this combination is cheaper than installing fibre all the way to the customer premises. Unlike most cable systems, this hybrid allows two-way communication.

Other technological innovations that can be used for educational communication in developing regions include:

i) Internet telephony : Packetised voice communication can be transmitted very inexpensively over the internet. Schools with internet access may be able to use their networks for voice communications as well (regulations vary by country). Using internet protocols for voice and data is much less expensive than using regular telephone networks.

ii) Community radio: Small community radio broadcasting stations can be important news sources for the community and can be used to broadcast educational radio programmes for listening in school, at home, or in community centres. Some school and telecentre projects are combining computer facilities with community radio stations, so that information received via the internet can be communicated more widely. Portable wind-up or solar-powered radio receivers are practical for school and community use.

Internet Service Provider (ISP) should provide local connectivity so that long distance calling charges are not incurred. However, in many rural and developing regions, local access is not available. The speed of access to the internet depends not only on the bandwidth available to reach the ISP, but also the number of ports at the ISP and the bandwidth it has available to reach an internet gateway. In addition to asking the ISP for such information, it is useful to check with other customers to determine whether they experience outages or delays, and whether they have noticed any improvement or degradation in access over time.

Batched and compressed e-mail accounts: Users can save money in telecommunications charges if they can compose messages off-line and send and receive e-mail in batches to the internet service provider (ISP).

Operating System Considerations of Software

Software, an essential component of computer systems, enables the hardware to do useful work for users. Educational computer systems for software is organised into the following four broad categories:

i) operating system (OS) software for client and server computers;
ii) basic computer application software, including software for word processing, spreadsheets, presentations, and graphics;
iii) educational software applications; and
iv) internet-related and -delivered software, including browsers, Java applications, and interactive tools on websites.

If Apple computers are purchased, then Apple's OS, which comes with the computer, will likely be used on client computers. If computers with Intel or Intel-compatible CPUs are purchased, the computers likely will come with a version of the Microsoft Windows OS. In contrast, decisions about what software should be used to operate networked computers are not as easy or predetermined as they are with client system software.

Basic Apple and Windows operating system software comes with the capability to enable computers to be connected together to manage small networks. However, larger and more robust networks that may need to be managed securely will require special network operating system software installed on the network's server to manage the functions of the network, including links to printers and other peripherals, e-mail, file sharing, security functions, and communication among linked computers.

For education systems, the education functions that need to be supported and the needs of students and teachers are the most important factors in making technology decisions. If the software and hardware solutions do not ultimately serve the teaching and learning process, then even "inexpensive" or "free" options can be very costly educationally. If key educational software programmes cannot be used on computer systems with "free" Open Source Software (OSS), then the "free" solution could become very expensive. Linux is also the first or second most popular operating system software for internet servers-accounting for about 30 per cent of all web servers in the world today.

The technical benefits of operating system and network operating system software generally are discussed in terms of the software's reliability, performance, scalability, security, and cost. A variety of comparisons have shown that servers running Linux crash less often and perform better than commercial and other OSS software. Also, Linux can be used on a wider range of computer platforms than any other operating system and is more secure than commercial OSS.

Operating system and network operating system software only account for about 5 per cent to 8 per cent of the total cost of buying a client computer system. In contrast, the ongoing costs to train teachers to integrate technology into teaching and learning, and to support and keep computer systems running from year to year, can be many times greater than the original purchase cost of the computer and the operating system or network operating system software.

In many cases, school systems will spend as much in two years for operating school computers as was spent initially to purchase and install a system that is expected to last five years. Therefore, it is more important to consider the total cost of ownership carefully—acquiring, installing, configuring, supporting, maintaining, training users in, using, and upgrading the software—when evaluating the real costs of using different types of operating or network operating system software. It is also important to emphasise that total cost of ownership studies carried out for corporations cannot and should not be used to justify purchase decisions for educational systems. There are special and critical differences between the needs and uses of computers in education and corporations. The most important factor in realising the potential educational benefits of technology is how teachers and students use computers and the internet in learning activities. Consequently, the most important cost factors in total cost of ownership studies of technology in education are linked to the use of technology and its integration into teaching and learning.

Therefore, when evaluating the use of OSS in education, it is essential to assess how different software decisions will affect how teachers and students use technology and how easy or difficult it may be for them to integrate it into routine teaching and learning.

Some countries, such as Namibia, may have greater technical capacity to manage UNIX and Linux operating systems than Microsoft NT, so using Linux could be a more cost-effective decision for them. Windows is the operating system used on 80 per cent to 90 per cent of all client computers in business, government, and the non-profit sectors of the economy. If students were to use computers in schools with OSS, some likely would not gain the needed skills and experience with Windows that prospective employers would demand.

Therefore, total cost of ownership calculations for education systems considering OSS would need to consider the costs that students and companies would likely incur to train workers to use Windows.

The lack of educational software applications that can operate on OSS, and the loss of current investment in Windows applications that could not be used on OSS, without using emulation software, would need to be considered as well in total cost of ownership calculations. Furthermore, many schools, especially those in developing countries, have very small budgets to purchase additional software for their computer systems. A shift to OSS would make some current investments useless, and replacing the software with versions to run on OSS, if they were available, would drain scarce resources. Also, some critical applications, such as software used in special-needs education, are not available for the OSS operating system, and a shift to OSS could prevent some students and schools from using their computers.

All computers in schools require a basic set of software applications to be useful for computer literacy programmes and to be integrated effectively into routine education programmes. These applications generally include software for word processing and manipulating numeric data such as spreadsheets, presentation software, and graphics software, and the increasingly important software to create websites and HTML documents.

Major commercial applications often are purchased because they are the types of software used in businesses and government offices, and it is often important to prepare students to use computers and applications that are common in the workforce. Where funding is a constraint, schools have the option of using Sun Microsystems public domain software application suite, called OpenOffice.

It includes an integrated graphical interface similar to MS-Office and WordPerfect and comprises word processing, spreadsheet, and presentation applications. StarOffice also has support for AutoPilot Web page design software, 3D graphics, diagrams, HTML editing, and calendar, newsgroup, browser, e-mail and scheduler, photo editing, and other applications. This software is also available in a variety of languages and can be downloaded for free from the internet.

There are versions of StarOffice for Windows and Linux operating systems. Thousands of software applications have been developed over the years, many for free, to meet specific educational objectives, including:

i) strengthening subject matter competence;

ii) providing drill and practice activities for different subjects;

iii) enhancing logical thinking and problem-solving skills;

iv) enriching research and writing activities;

v) simulating complex or dangerous processes that enable students to change variables and visualise how processes are changed; and providing opportunities for students to extend learning beyond the scope of classroom activities.

As with all uses of computers to enhance and improve teaching and learning, the key to success is not the type of educational software that is used, but how teachers use the software and integrate it into their teaching programmes.

Significant benefits to teaching and learning can be achieved without using any specialised educational software. However, when used effectively by teachers, many excellent educational software applications can enhance the use of computers in education. Achieving these benefits is not guaranteed, and the costs of purchasing, often very expensive software, must be considered carefully.

Selecting software should not be done based on the publishers' promotional materials. Rather, schools and teachers should seek out evaluations of software from other educators to learn the benefits of and possible problems with the software.

Numerous websites can provide evaluations of educational software. Also, publishers often will provide evaluation copies of software that teachers can use to test the products before the school decides to purchase them. When evaluating educational software, teachers and schools need to develop evaluation criteria so that purchase decisions are based on objective and subjective measures of educational quality.

One of the most important benefits of internet- and web-related software is that most of it can be used regardless of the hardware and software installed at schools. The "platform independence" of the internet reduces the costs involved in using the internet in education and enhances its benefits. One key area of internet use is access to a variety of internet and web-based software applications, much of it freely available in different languages that can be used by teachers and students in a variety of ways, including:

i) browser and search software that enables students to carry out research on the internet and engage in enquiry-based learning activities using the millions of websites on the internet;
ii) e-mail software that allows users to send and receive communication from other learners and websites; listserv or e-mail distribution software that allows groups of users to form and communicate easily by e-mail;
iii) web-based discussion forum software that allows users to engage in ongoing dialogues in which the topics or themes are linked to form discussion threads;
iv) interactive web-based publishing tools that allow students and teachers to publish their thoughts, comments, experiences, pictures, suggestions, etc.;
v) internet- and web-based chat and instant messaging software that allows users to engage in live text-based discussions;
vi) easy-to-use web page construction and publishing tools;
vii) voice and video software applications that allow teachers and students to participate in synchronous audio- and videoconferencing, if sufficient bandwidth is available; and
viii) file storage and retrieval software that allows users to share digital files easily, including documents, presentations, images, data, and music, with other users.

The existence of these online or web-based software applications that enable users to communicate at a distance has given rise to opportunities for collaborative and project-based learning that were not possible before the internet. Since learning is very much a social activity, the ability to link students and teachers together to form learning communities can significantly enhance learning outcomes and opportunities to develop lifelong learning skills.

Another important category of internet-related software includes applications, many of which are freely available, that enable teachers and students to construct and publish web pages and HTML documents on the internet. In addition, the internet's "platform independence" helped give rise to a variety of software applications, including JAVA, FLASH, and Shockwave, which can be used to create learning applications that simulate simple and complex processes and concepts.

Distance Learning Video Techniques

Implicit in the term "distance learning" is the concept of education that can occur without the need for the instructor and student to be present in the same location at the same time. Distance learning is the application of video networking to education at all levels, including higher education, continuing education, and corporate training, as well as military and government training. There are some potential benefits that flow from implementing a distance learning environment. Distance learning has the been shown to produce the following potential benefits:

i) *Reduced learning time:* Typically 30-40 per cent less time is required for learning to be achieved compared to classroom instruction.
ii) *On-demand learning:* Instruction is available when and where the learner needs it, eliminating the need to wait for, or travel to, a scheduled class. In addition, distance learning increases access to learning for the disabled.
iii) *Increased motivation:* Students frequently report that they find technology-based interactive learning more interesting and enjoyable than classroom lectures.
iv) *Increased achievement:* When corrective feedback or a learning strategy designed to help students achieve mastery in a certain area is provided, students often show better test results, retention, or job performance from technology-based interactive learning.

v) *Better quality control:* Since learning experiences are delivered in the same way each time, they are much more consistent and reliable than classroom instruction.

vi) *Increased safety:* Students can learn about dangerous procedures with reduced safety concerns.

vii) *Greater flexibility:* Fluctuations in the number of learners, or their backgrounds, can be accommodated more easily than with classroom instruction.

viii) *Improved accountability:* Automatic collection of data on learner performance can verify that learning has been accomplished and identify learning problems.

ix) *Faster revision:* Learning experiences are delivered via a networked system, simplifying the process of making changes and updates to the curriculum.

x) *Reduced delivery costs:* Once developed, technology-based interactive learning is likely to cost less when compared to traditional, labour-intensive classroom instruction.

xi) *Learner controlled:* Each learner is able to review topics or to skip the information they already know.

Distance education refers to teaching and learning situations in which the instructor and the learner are geographically separated, and therefore rely on electronic devices and print materials for instructional delivery. Distance education includes distance teaching—the instructor's role in the process, and distance learning—the student's role in the process. The fundamental method to unite the distance teacher and the distance learner is the network—technology that bridges the gap between the teacher and the learner.

Networks suitable for distance learning come in many shapes and sizes, including everything from satellite transmission systems to long-haul, state-wide fibre optic networks. One of the key issues to be addressed when designing a network to support a distance learning environment is the capability for operation in a heterogeneous environment. This stems from the fact that most distance learning environments span significant geographical distances, and typically present network implementers with a mixture of delivery systems that offer widely varied capabilities.

A large distance learning deployment may span territories that require the integration of disparate technologies, including T1, Integrated Service Digital Network (ISDN), Asynchronous Transfer Mode (ATM), Frame Relay, and Ethernet into a unified content delivery system. Since the underlying characteristics of the network transmission technologies all have different capabilities, it is important to match the format of the content to the delivery system.

Video Tape is the cornerstone technology of distance learning environments, and is the key data type to be transmitted if instruction is to be successful. Video transmissions can be categorised in many ways, but there are three key types of video content:

i) *Video On Demand*: The ability of a distance learner to access educational content that is stored on the network on a video server. The content may be video of a lecture that a student could not physically attend because of a scheduling conflict, or a session that was recorded in a studio for the express purpose of on-demand transmission as part of standard coursework.

ii) *Live Broadcast Video*: The ability of a distance teacher to deliver a lecture or other educational session directly into a video camera for real-time broadcast to distance learners across the network. Programming can also be simultaneously copied and stored by a video server to facilitate the needs of students unavailable at the actual lecture time. These students can then access the material as a video-on-demand session as described above.

iii) *Videoconferencing*: The ability of distance learners and distance teachers to participate in a two-way interactive educational environment. Video cameras must be employed at all points of the videoconference to allow this two-way interactivity to occur, and the network must be able to support real-time data transfer in both directions. Videoconferencing recreates the typical classroom environment, even though participants may be miles, or countries, apart.

The quality of educational video transmission is a critical success factor in establishing a distance learning environment. Regardless of the type of video that is being transmitted—live broadcast, video-on-demand, or videoconferencing—the quality of the video is a key determinant in the knowledge transfer between the video teacher and the video learner. Video is streamed from either a broadcast server or a video disc server in one direction from the server to the distance learners. The nature of one-way noninteractive video allows for some buffering of video at the edge of the network, enabling the underlying latency and inconsistency of the transmitting network to be smoothed out. Video is transmitted in both directions simultaneously between the student and the teacher.

The real-time, two-way interactive nature of this type of video traffic requires transport by a network with very low underlying latency and inconsistency, and tolerates little or no delay-inducing buffering of video within the network itself. The science of transmitting video across networks is essentially the science of compression.

Distance education implies that learning will take place over a wide geographical area, spanning both LAN and WAN network technologies. Compression and transmission solutions must be capable of delivery over the widest range of network technologies. The H.320 standard for videoconferencing has been in existence for several years, and the majority of videoconferencing systems adhere to this standard. Video Coder-Decoder (CODEC) manufacturers such as PictureTel, VTEL, and Zydacron use this standard. H.320 videoconferencing can be implemented over a very wide range of networking technologies, including ISDN, ATM, T1, and E3, supporting deployment in distance learning applications that span the globe. The H.320 standard also provides scalable bandwidth utilisation to support delivery of very high quality, two-way interactive video transmission at speeds of 128 Kbps, 384 Kbps, 768 Kbps, and 1.5 Mbps.

A key advantage of H.320 is that it supports dial-up connectivity to virtually all videoconferencing systems installed worldwide. This is essential in distance learning environments, as it delivers connectivity to experts from educational institutions across the globe with a dial-up procedure as simple as using a telephone. H.320 provides high-quality images at any speed from 384 Kbps and up—its unique ability to support a range of speeds lends itself well to the disparate nature of the distance learning environment. This flexibility enables an educator to present a real-time lecture to hundreds of students in dozens of locations across an ISDN-based WAN at 384 Kbps, and moments later conduct a conference with an on-campus student across the ATM LAN at 25 Mbps.

There are several alternatives to H.320 videoconferencing, including:

a) *MPEG-2:* Also referred to as H.310 when implemented over ATM, Motion Pictures Expert Group-2 (MPEG-2) provides very high quality videoconferencing. MPEG-2 is a compression system that requires the underlying network to provide 6 to 8 Mbps of transmission bandwidth. These extensive bandwidth requirements limit implementation of MPEG-2 to restricted geographies that can support high data transport rates. In reality, MPEG-2 can only be implemented over Fast Ethernet or ATM in LAN environments, and is dependent on the availability of extensive long-haul fibre optic connections in WAN deployments. MPEG-2 is growing in popularity with the current emphasis on high-quality distance learning applications.

b) *Motion JPEG:* This is another compression technique that provides very high quality videoconferencing. Motion Joint Photographic Experts Group (M-JPEG) also requires very high bandwidth-8 to 12 Mbps, making it critical that the end user has ample bandwidth on the network to support the application.

c) *H.323:* This new technology is designed to implement videoconferencing over Transmission Control Protocol/ Internet Protocol (TCP/IP) networks. This method of supporting videoconferencing shows great promise in terms of its ability to deliver video over a wide range of network types and architectures. It is challenged, however, in its ability to deliver video of the required quality—a critical success factor in distance duration. The best-effort nature of router-based long-haul TCP/IP networks simply does not deliver video with the consistency or quality required for successful distance training.

MPEG-1 is the video compression standard of choice for implementing one-way non-interactive video transmissions in distance learning environments. MPEG-1 uses a compression approach that relates the video information on a given frame to the frames that surround it. Computations are made to determine what has changed from one frame to the next, and only the changed video is sent across the network. This approach yields high levels of compression with excellent image resolution. The transmission rate of MPEG-1 is approximately 1.2 Mbps, rendering it suitable to transport on all LAN types and to a wide range of WANs as well. MPEG-1 has been widely implemented as a compression technology, and is the default format for commercially available educational video content. MPEG-1 is well suited to delivering content in both video-on-demand applications and live broadcast video applications.

E-LEARNING INDUSTRY

Today, e-learning industry is still quite small in terms of revenues, but is populated with literally hundreds of companies already and more are jumping into the tray everyday. E-learning companies are difficult to categorise because they offer such a wide range of products and services to a number of different target markets, using several different revenue models. While the core competency of these companies did not change with the advent of the internet age, their methods of reaching their customers had to if they were to address issues such as scalability, access, and timeliness. The traditional model of educating people via a live instructor lacked all three of these characteristics; an individual can only teach so many people at a time, is not available anytime and anywhere to the learner, and may not be up to date with the most recent information. E-learning fits the three characteristics:

i) It can be scaled almost infinitely,

ii) it is available anywhere there is an internet connection; and

iii) it can be continually updated with new information relevant to the learner.

One of the major opportunities for e-learning companies is to provide both the advanced and remedial coursework via online learning that high schools may not be equipped to offer because of constraints in both the number of teachers and gaps in teacher proficiency. Schools will need to hire more than two million teachers over the next ten years, but the coming wave of baby-boomer retirements will make this difficult. Particularly in the areas of math, science and technology, schools are finding it more and more difficult to offer salaries that are even remotely competitive with the private sector. E-learning, therefore, may become a more valuable tool for students as teachers become ever scarcer resources. Schools are increasingly turning to technology to help with both the organisational aspects of managing the academic careers of their students and with curriculum development. Sophisticated student information systems and even more extensive enterprise resource planning (ERP) systems not only help with the day-to-day management of a school district, but also help keep track of and analyse students' educational records. Systems like these can be useful in highlighting areas of weakness so individual students can receive help before it is too late.

These tools can also be valuable in keeping parents apprised of assignments, tests, activities, and overall progress. In addition, services and tools exist today that can help a school precisely map its curriculum to state learning standards in order to achieve accountability requirements.

The parents may become ready purchasers of e-learning products. Whether for formal homeschooling purposes or simply supplemental learning, we believe parents are looking for more types of academic products and services to aid in their child's education. Many parents are starting to teach their children to use technology at a very early age and are looking for appropriate educational applications for kids from preschool through high school. Whether the child needs remedial help in a particular subject to keep up with classmates or is looking for more advanced resources, the web has a bounty of educational offerings. The parent groups will be strong supporters of schools implementing web-based tools that will enable parents to better keep up with their child's progress through monitoring assignments and grades and communication with teachers.

In US, technology companies such as Intel and Microsoft have launched major initiatives to get technology into schools through donations of hardware and software, and also to train teachers to use the new tools in the classroom. US businesses know that in order to retain their leadership positions in the world market, their future employees must get an early start in learning how to use technology.

E-learning is gaining on traditional instructor-led training (ILT) in the corporate environment. Although ILT currently represents more than 70 per cent of delivered training, this percentage is expected to fall to 35-40 per cent by 2004.

Replacing it is technology-based training, the largest component of which will be e-learning. Radical improvements in offerings, an insatiable demand for IT skills, the extension of the enterprise, and government sponsorship wilt each spark the growth of e-learning in corporations.

In US, these company offers, extensive learning opportunities through their websites that are designed to make customers more comfortable with their purchase. Even those courses that are not directly aimed at selling a product or service benefit the company by strengthening brand names and creating goodwill among clients by virtue of offering free educational opportunities. As products and services grow increasingly complicated, that learning will become a large component of developing brands and maintaining customer relationships.

Today, many of these people are currently participating in informal learning activities on the internet. We believe that some lifelong learners are turning to more formal learning experiences in the form of courses as these types of resources become more abundant and sophisticated. Whether people want to learn how to cook, get a refresher on Shakespearean literature, or read a primer on the wildlife in a particular region, the internet is likely to have a multitude of offerings. We believe that as broadband internet connections become more prevalent in households, enabling more interactive learning experiences, this type of recreational learning will become more commonplace, for entertainment as well as educational purposes.

This type of learning is generally avocational, the prices consumers are willing to pay will likely be lower than for "required" work- or academic-related online learning. In fact, we believe that much of the e-learning that consumers end up participating in will be provided by businesses at little or no charge to them. Learning opportunities being used as a marketing tool by companies to promote their products or services.

The "lifelong learning" opportunities, including professional continuing education in the consumer market because we believe that although continuing education is typically work-related, those participating in it are, in most cases, personally responsible for the purchase and completion of the courses. That is to say, even though they may be reimbursed by an employer, people taking continuing education are typically professionals of some kind who do not necessarily work in an organisation that has a separate training department. Therefore, these individuals are likely to make purchase decisions based on their own unique needs and circumstances.

APPLICATIONS OF TECHNOLOGY-BASED EDUCATION

Throughout the 1970s and 1980s, technical innovation brought increasingly diverse and more powerful technological tools into schools. Early studies sought to demonstrate the impact of technologies or software on student learning and they were tied very specifically to the particular technologies used by the subjects of the study. These technologies were typically text-based, locally networked or stand-alone computer-assisted instruction applications. As these technologies have become outdated and replaced by graphics-rich and networked environments, the studies that looked at impact on students have been outdated themselves.

Technologies can play in addressing the key challenges of teaching and learning. The pace of both technological development and the introduction of new technologies into educational settings has dramatically accelerated during the past decade. The combination of computation, connectivity, visual and multimedia capacities, miniaturisation, and speed have radically changed the potential for technologies in schooling.

These developments are now making it possible for technologies to be designed and deployed to produce powerful and linked technologies that can substantially address some of the core problems of education. For example, there are currently existing technologies that are ideally suited to ameliorating problems like teacher isolation, access to rich and substantial resources, and parent involvement in schooling.

Teacher practices, student experiences, pedagogical contexts, and even what was actually being done with the computers—all of these factors were bracketed out. The specific kinds of technology applications, such as integrated learning systems, could improve students' scores on tests of discrete information and skills, such as spelling, basic mathematics, geographical place names, and so on. In order to be effective, innovative and robust technological resources must be used to support systematic changes in educational environments that take into account simultaneous changes in administrative procedures, curriculum, time and space constraints, school-community relationships, and a range of other logistical and social factors.

Technologies may contribute to student learning, there has been increasing recognition that technology is a crucial player in a more complex process of change that cannot be accomplished by technological fixes alone. The changing and improving the circumstances of teaching and learning are much more holistic than those measured by most standard assessment practices, and they require more sophisticated strategies of the researcher who is attempting to capture and analyse them. To explore how best to use technology in the service of these goals requires looking at technology use in context, and gaining an understanding of how technology use is mediated by factors such as the organisation of the classroom, the pedagogical methods of the teacher, and the sociocultural setting of the school.

The most pervasive of the technologies with educational applications are the internet and World Wide Web, but other technologies can also be used to facilitate adult learning. In considering the role of technology in adult learning, adult educators are faced with a number of challenges, including how to respond to technology and how to exploit it without diminishing the learning experience.

The integrating technology into adult learning is to use it as means for instructional delivery. In basic skills instruction, an example of this approach is the individualised learning system (ILS). ILSs are designed to provide instruction and practice in a set of subskills that together form an entire curriculum. Other examples include televised instruction and instruction delivered through video or audiotapes. Although this approach lends itself to individualising instruction, for the most part, the learner works in isolation from other learners and, in some instances, the teacher. For example, ILSs require learners only to retrieve the software programme, identify themselves, and employ a limited number of keystrokes.

Technology is frequently used to complement instruction and extend learning, in adult learning settings. In adult basic education, for example, a learner might use a piece of software to practice a weak or underdeveloped skill area that has been the focus of classroom instruction. Another example of this approach is the use of internet activities and assignments to supplement traditional distance learning. In this approach, the instructor remains the primary coordinator of instruction and the extent to which technology is integrated with traditional instruction depends upon both the teacher's style and the kind and type of technology available.

Use of technology to complement instruction extends the instruction beyond the knowledge and experiences of the teacher and can also provide opportunities for the teacher to learn. The approach also provides learners the opportunity to practice skills in private, and it can promote self-direction by allowing learners to supplement instruction in ways that meet their individual needs. A major limitation of this approach is the kind and type of material available that is suitable for adults and that promotes good adult learning practices. In the case of software, for example, teachers must take time to locate, review, and select software packages. Also, drill and practice, which does not involve the development of high-level cognitive skills such as problem solving, is the focus of many software programmes. The cost of acquiring the most suitable software may also be a limitation.

As an instructional tool, technology is integrated into instructional activities. The primary instructional goals and outcomes remain the same, but technology is used to enrich and extend them. Although acquiring technology-related skills is not the primary focus in this approach, instructional activities frequently support their development. In completing writing assignments, for example, learners develop skills in word processing.

The spread of the internet and the World Wide Web has made this approach very common in distance education and in other education and training settings. Technology has also been used to extend adult literacy curricula in a multilevel classroom by enabling learners to have immediate access to internet-based resources that provide content of interest to their life situations and allow for teaching of skills in context. This approach allows learners to develop skills and have experiences with technology in ways that will benefit them outside the instructional setting.

When used as an instructional tool, the internet provides access to information and resources that might not ordinarily be available. In adult basic education, a shortage of curricular resources that integrate and benefit from technology exists. Access to technology for either educational providers or learners can also be a problem. Like any other instructional tool, technology can serve to perpetuate poor educational practice or it can become a means for transforming learning. In formal learning settings, leadership for using technology effectively rests with the instructor.

Technology can enhance adult learning because it has the potential to increase flexibility, provide access to expertise, facilitate discussion among learners who cannot meet face to face, reduce feelings of isolation often experienced by non-traditional learners, increase learner autonomy, and support and promote constructivist and collaborative learning. However, because "technology in and of itself does not promote learning", its use does not obviate the educator's responsibility for structuring the learning to ensure these benefits result.

The transformative differentiator for the next generation is the programmability of interconnected networks. With increases in software programmability, we increase interactivity, increase communication, increase learner adaptability, increase shared visualisations, increase shared laboratory access, and increase experiential learning.

The technology objective is to construct a safe environment for the child while engaged in technology-driven learning experiences. For real world interactions, video playbacks of children engaged in learning activities are frequent and reviewed by student, teacher and parent. Technology networks kids together in groups to learn and practise their combined skills. Whether children are working on art or science, they work with embedded technology that measures their performance. Students use wearable technologies to exchange, collect, communicate and present information either posted to large screen displays, or holographic 3D environments. As they collect information, it automatically maps to the learning objectives for their skill group and displays cumulative data about the group's success in onscreen graphics for easy monitoring. Anonymity is crucial, as performance indicators supplant grades.

Teachers help students enhance screen literacy skills by building interactive multimedia for reuse among other learning populations worldwide. Teachers share their activities, thoughts, and technology ideas with a virtual team of experts in business, higher education and other institutions. Teachers are mentors, still using their nurturing techniques in the learning spaces to socialise children. In addition, each child has his own virtual mentor that can be accessed anytime. The mentor follows the children's activities online, suggesting new ideas and dialoguing interactively to understand the student's emotions and competencies. When children go online, the experience is secure and private.

Online content is filtered by the virtual mentor, who constantly reports noteworthy events to the parents, teachers and other interested parties. Embedded assessment is constantly sent to the teacher, parent and mentor. The virtual mentor consistently maps to performance goals and adjusts student activities to keep kids more focused on learning rather than relying on test taking. Parents can participate in their children's activities wherever they are via wireless mobile video computing and emerging communication technologies.

The most advanced and most desirable technology is the creation of a tele-immersive environment for teaching and learning. This is a three-dimensional virtual space, which mimics the real space both visually, aurally and tactually. It is one in which both the student/apprentice and teacher/master can meet and interact. This technology does not exist yet but it is very feasible from what we know today.

In this new world, computers have long been a powerful tool for education. At the same time, the internet has brought an unprecedented level of great educational content to a wide audience, encouraging teachers to share curriculums and resources worldwide. E-mail has facilitated improved communication among administrators, teachers, students, parents and educational researchers, and emerging web services technologies will create further opportunities for collaborative learning.

Increased industry and government funding in learning science promises to vastly improve the ways technology is applied to learning. Solving business problems with computers looks easy when compared to the often complex and little-understood process of learning. And technology is only part of the solution. All the computers in the world will not make a difference without enthusiastic students, skilled and committed teachers, involved and informed parents, and a society that underscores the value of lifelong learning.

Simulation technologies and powerful sensor technologies provide scaleable models for engaging in the learning by doing. Simulations allow students the opportunity to build integrated environments with objects in one environment that serve similar purposes in another environment. This level of programmability across multiple visual environments is the metric for successful development.

Computer-based simulation has been used extensively in the airline industry and in the military for effective training of cognitive, perceptual and motor skills. More recently, simulators have been used for training medical personnel in procedures using manikins and virtual reality systems.

Medical simulators may include both three-dimensional (3D) models of human anatomy displayed on a computer monitor coupled with a "haptics" device that conveys a sense of touch to the user. Thus, a paramedic inserting a chest tube or a surgeon cutting into a 'virtual' patient can visualise the anatomy and feel the forces associated with the actual procedure using a force feedback device similar to the controllers used in computer gaming.

In medicine, the development of performance metrics and the objective assessment of performance is a difficult and complex process, because it requires decomposing the medical procedures into their elemental parts using a process called task analysis, depends on 'buy-in' from experts in the medical community, and requires validation using rigorous scientific methods. One approach for refreshing and sustaining technical skills is to allow the medic and other health care personnel to practise procedures in simulated environments that reproduce many of the difficulties found in real world, emergency settings.

These new learning systems will change the process of learning, redefine the role played by the teachers, and create an enormous range of challenging new teaching occupations. What they will not do is replace the need for human teachers, tutors and counsellors who can provide expert instruction, provide inspiration, encouragement and discipline, and serve as exemplars of the kinds of expertise a learner can aspire to achieve. Teaching and other related occupations in education and training systems will become much more like other "knowledge economy" professions, having more opportunities for professional growth and more support from technology and specialists.

Today, modern physicians can draw on an enormous array of medical professionals to provide specialised expertise, develop and maintain sophisticated medical equipment and software, and perform elaborate testing. It would be down-right frightening if your medical care was limited to what your family physician could perform in his office, but that is largely the situation teachers find themselves in today.

New learning systems will enable teachers to create challenging assignments that can close the gap between the world of instruction and the world of work and tailor instruction to increase the efficiency of learning. New learning systems will make more productive use of both the teacher's and learner's time and talents, and provide useful, multidimensional assessments of each learner's expertise and ability to accomplish complex tasks.

Next generation learning systems will allow learners to access live and recorded lectures from multiple sources. Performance-based assignments will allow learners and small groups to demonstrate levels of expertise in tasks where they are strongly motivated to succeed. Learning systems will be built from a set of powerful tools allowing instructional designers to go from concept to operational systems quickly. They will also permit continuous upgrades and improvements as problems are discovered and new concepts are proposed and tested.

The tools will include systems for continuously evaluating the learner's approach to expertise in critical areas; providing quick, context-sensitive, individualised responses to questions by dispatching questions to automated systems and human tutors and experts; rapidly building networks of learners and teachers; monitoring a user's level of interest, anxiety and motivation; adapting to specific learners; and systems for building simulations reflecting the state-of-the-art in science, engineering and other fields.

Teachers and learners will be able to call on a variety human tutors, counsellors and experts and summon a variety of automated help systems for addressing routine questions. Learners will work face-to-face with teachers and tutors and be able to call on a worldwide network of subject-matter experts and other specialists when interesting questions arise. Sophisticated tools will help diagnose sources of confusion and suggest new learning strategies based on analysis of the experience of large numbers of learners facing similar situations.

In the future, education and training institutions and their supporting industries must dramatically improve the way they invest in innovation, manage innovation, invest in capital equipment and assign responsibilities to different occupations. These changes will reshape the nature of employment in education in a number of ways:

i) Teaching will become much more personalised because teachers will be able to spend much more time in dialogues with individuals and small groups.

ii) The roles bundled in the job of today's teachers are likely to be "unbundled" with many tasks performed by experts or automated systems with specialised expertise.

iii) As a consequence, teachers and tutors working directly with learners will work as a part of a sophisticated and continuously changing team involving specialists and speciality firms. Professionals may specialise as subject-matter experts, expert teachers, instructional designers, courseware developers, applications designers, or a variety of other occupations, and they may concentrate on the roles at which they excel and find most rewarding.

iv) The new supporting industries will generate an enormous number of new occupational opportunities. Many of these will be in firms that produce tools and services sold to a large number of education and training institutions worldwide. Since many of the skills involved will be required by other businesses, movement into and out of education professions is likely.

v) Professionals at all levels will need to continuously upgrade their skills and use an array of tools for professional development throughout their careers. This can include keeping abreast of developments in the field being taught, understanding advances in the theory of cognition, pedagogy and assessment, and understanding innovations in software design, standards and communications.

The improvements in teaching and learning just described will require a major national investment in research and skilful management of these innovations by education and training institutions. Making effective use of these tools and redefining the roles of teachers and other professionals needed to use them to achieve real gains in learning will require creative management by education and training institutions and supporting industries. The challenging new occupations of teaching, tool building and support services will give education occupations the same respect, and same remuneration, enjoyed by other knowledge professionals.

This new education environment will incorporate 3D computer animation and graphics, real-time image rendering, multichannel immersive audio, video, text, and haptics. Techniques that promote a high degree of student attention, goal attainment motivation, and satisfaction will be adapted from approaches already much better understood and employed by the gaming industry. New multimedia and internet technologies are creating novel ways to teach and learn through this very process of creating new ways to see, hear, and touch.

The future of education will be profoundly affected by forthcoming information technology. But even more importantly, it will be affected by how educators and students use the technology to prepare for lifelong learning in the face of unrelenting change.

REFERENCES

Burge, E. J, and N. M, Carter, "It's Building, But Is It Designing? Constructing Internet-Based Learning Environments", Paper presented at the 18th World Conference of the International Council for Distance Education, University Park, PA, June 2-6, 1997.

______________ and J. M, Roberts, *Classrooms with a Difference: A Practical Guide to the Use of Conferencing Technologies*, Toronto: Distance Learning Office, Ontario Institute for Studies in Education, 1993.

Cahoon, B., "Teaching and Learning Internet Skills", In *Adult Learning and the Internet*, edited by B. Cahoon, pp. 5-13, *New Directions for Adult and Continuing Education*, no. 78, San Francisco: Jossey-Bass, 1998.

Forsyth, I., "Teaching and Learning Materials and the Internet" (2nd ed.), London: Kogan Page, 1998.

Khan, B. H., "Discussion of resources and attributes of the Web for the creation of meaningful learning environments", *Cyber Psychology and Behaviour*, 3(1), 17-23, 2000.

Rapaport, M., *Computer Mediated Communications: Bulletin Boards, Computer Conferencing, Electronic Mail, and Information Retrieval*, New York: John Wiley & Sons, 1991.

Roberts, L., "A Transformation of Learning: Use of the NII for Education and Lifelong Learning", In D. P. Ely & B. B. Minor (eds.), *Educational Media and Technology Yearbook 1995/1996*, pp. 50-66, Englewood, CO: Libraries Unlimited, 1996.

3

Web-based Pedagogical Learning

A pedagogical technique is defined as a manner of accomplishing teaching objectives. These pedagogical techniques are classified as one-alone techniques, one-to-one techniques, one-to-many techniques, and many-to-many techniques. These techniques can be used to facilitate adult learning. However, there are many constraints that limit the opportunities for online utilisation. Among these are the type of institutions, geographical issues, equipments, resources, course timeframe, course workload, communication pattern, and the financial health of the programme provider. The programme must comply to the rules, regulations, and policies of the institution and these may vary considerably from a private to a public institution, and from secondary education to universities.

Lack of computer resources, such as hardware, software, and communication networks though is an important limitation for many online programmes. Employers may have changing expectations regarding technology based learning and students may have changing learning preferences as they begin to have experience with online courses in non-instructional environments. Further, the local community, faculty, staff, and students all have demands to the programme.

The structure of distance teaching is determined to a considerable degree by the principles of industrialisation, particularly by those of rationalisation, division of labour, and mass production; the teaching process is gradually restructured through increasing mechanisation and mass production. Major elements for defining distance education dealt with the separation of teacher and learner. This separation does not necessarily imply much freedom of study location. Many distance education programmes, for instance, those taught by videoconferencing, require students to attend classes at fixed locations.

In computer-mediated communication (CMC), one must distinguish between synchronous and asynchronous communication. In asynchronous communication, the message is stored in the communication medium until the receivers find it convenient to retrieve it. Synchronous communication, on the other hand, is inflexible, but allows people to communicate in real time, as they do face-to-face or on the telephone. Scheduling of synchronous communication varies in flexibility.

Distance education programmes may allow students to communicate whenever it is convenient for them. Students may prefer to study during the weekends, after their children have gone to bed, during regular work hours, or whenever they have time available. CMC could be completely independent of time. Ideally it is available 24 hours a day, 365 days a year.

Distance education programmes could provide students with access to several media or sources of information: print, video, face-to-face meetings, computer conferencing, etc. This approach will support different learning styles and prevent exclusion of students lacking access to or knowledge of high technology media. CMC can easily and favourably be supplemented by or integrated with textbooks, audio and video conferences, computer-aided instruction, etc., and it is to some extent an administrative choice to decide how much a course should rely on CMC for communication and content delivery.

Cooperation can be hard to achieve in distance education. A major problem for many students is the loneliness that results from limited access to student peers; the urge for individual freedom may intensify the problem. However, group communication technologies such as audio conferencing, video conferencing, and computer conferencing have been devised to facilitate cooperation at a distance. Many students have full-time jobs and families to take care of and many are reluctant to participate if it means relinquishing high-quality family life and job achievements.

E-learning stands at the crossroads of the information economy and the knowledge economy. While the internet generates an unwieldy excess of information, it also enables products that can empower workers, students, and private individuals to harness this information. The new form of education "e-learning", as it is the use of networked technology that will make the learning revolution possible. However, its name is less important than the role it will play in changing the way we work and live. Many people have touted the ability of e-learning to provide information to "anyone, anytime, anywhere". The true power of e-learning will be in its ability to bring the right information to the right people at the right time.

Network technology has enabled a proliferation of customised and timely educational tools that optimise investment in human capital: e-learning solutions facilitate the delivery of the right information and skills to the right people at the right time. The globalisation of the economy, shortage of skilled workers, free agent mentality, new flexible work situations and numerous other factors have created problems not easily solved by traditional education, spurring the initial growth of the e-learning industry.

Today, the main currency of the economy is unarguably information: information about customers, information about competitors, information about employees. It is a chicken-and-egg problem to determine whether the advent of the computer age brought about the proliferation of information, or if the need for information drove the rapid development of computer technology, but the fact remains that the computer age and the information age hatched at about the same time. However, even the notion of the information age, with its vast stores of computer-generated data locked away in inaccessible databases, is looking a bit antiquated. The major impact that the internet has already had on the world and its promise for the future is its ability to connect man and machines to one another so that information, whether it is stored in a brain or on a server, can be organised into meaningful knowledge bases that are readily accessible to those who can benefit from them.

In the information age, the knowledge age is still marked by the need for investment in human capital. The concepts of e-learning and knowledge management are beginning to organisation, but we believe that the characteristics of the "new economy" are making the need for these tools even more apparent.

The main benefits of using networked technology for learning are fairly obvious. The immediacy of information on the internet is an obvious advantage in comparison to the more traditional methods of information retrieval. It is certainly a lot easier to flip over to your internet browser and look up information on almost any subject in the world than it is to trek down to the local library and hope that they have a relevant book that is not checked out. To date, the internet has been used for primarily this type of learning: random seek-and-find events that are not connected to your previous or next learning experience.

The true power of e-learning lies not in the anyone, anyplace, anytime model, but rather in its potential to provide the right information to the right people at the right times and places. This is the yet-to-be-fulfilled promise of e-learning.

In future, that web-based integrated learning systems will revolutionise e-learning by enabling personalised, interactive, just-in-time, current, and user-centric learning tools. These systems will allow all facets of a course of study, including pre-assessment, learning modules completed, practice items, collaboration, and testing to be tracked.

Personalisation will be achieved by using small chunks of information, or learning objects, to assemble a course from the ground up using pre-existing templates. The reusability of these learning objects will make this level of customisation feasible in terms of both time and expense. These reusable learning objects, the interoperability of which will be based on a set of accepted industry standards, will be the key to the creation of an expansive learning economy. Today's technology-based learning is simply an extension of traditional textbook-based learning, where the user reads content from a screen instead of from a page.

Today's interaction generally consists of the learner being able to click on an unknown word for the definition on a linked page or the ability to play a short video clip. The manifestations of e-learning will truly engage the learner in a give-and-take type of learning that involves simulations of real-world events and sophisticated collaborations with other learners and the instructor. This will move education and training away from the "just-in-case" model in which learners engage in event-based sessions that require learning to take place outside of the context in which it will be used.

Technologies such as electronic performance support systems (EPSS) will allow users to receive training at the exact time and place that it is needed to complete a task. One of the most under-appreciated benefits of learning via networked technology, as opposed to earlier non-networked versions of technology-based training (like CD-ROMs or installed software), is its ability to always present uptodate material. It is relatively easy for the content provider to remotely change and update material on a web page based on new information or new needs of the learner. On the other hand, a CD-ROM is static, requiring a new product to be distributed anytime there is a change in the material.

E-learning introduces an entirely new model for learning—one that focuses primarily on the needs of the learner, instead of on the abilities of the instructor. With e-learning, the learner is able to participate in custom-fitted learning experiences that offer the exact material she needs in the form in which she learns best. The instructor, if there is one, goes from being the "sage on the stage" to the "guide on the side".

E-learning lends to the process of teaching is leverage of time and resources. In live collaborative learning environments, a teacher can only respond to so many students in a given amount of time. Also, the number of students that can participate in the class will be limited by those who can make the time. In a traditional learning environment, such as a college classroom, e-learning has the potential to greatly aid instructors in the organisation of a class. Web-based tools are now on the market that give an instructor the ability to centralise the management of a class on the web. Such a web-based forum allows the archival of notes (or even video files of lectures), communication with students outside of class, and possibly even the ability to monitor student performance.

In short, a set of e-learning standards must be developed and accepted by the vendor community. In order to achieve true sophistication in terms of understanding the objectives of a learner and addressing those objectives with a highly customised programme of learning, all of the components of a technology-based learning system must be speaking the same language. As learning is essentially the transfer of knowledge from one person to another, there will always be issues of intellectual property involved in the process of delivering instruction. Colleges and universities face this problem in dealing with the research products of faculty members, and e-learning vendors will have to deal with it as well.

WEB-BASED LEARNING APPROACHES

Effective web-based learning should include not just training in the use of technology. It must be integrated with pedagogical uses of technology to bring about learning for the development of lifelong learning skills and other emerging goals of education to meet the demands of the information age. Whenever web technology is used in educational settings, it is vital to reflect on how this affects students, faculty members, courses and institutions.

Web-based learning is seen by many as a transformative vehicle for increasing the pace of change and reform in higher education. For these and other reasons, analysis of quality assurance in web-based learning is an essential topic for education policy makers. The common problem now in the higher education sector is to identify an effective model to assure quality in the delivery of web-based learning that can fit the various stakeholders' expectations. The first stage for doing this is to identify the critical success factors that would contribute to quality assurance in web-based learning.

As the use of technology to facilitate and deliver distance learning courses has increased, new challenges have emerged for the administration, faculty, staff and students of universities developing and implementing distance learning programmes. Many faculties fear distance learning is just a means of reducing their ranks, or a means to solve budget problems. Others fear the dehumanisation and alienation of students as well as loss of critical thinking and social skills. On the other hand, rather than feeling threatened, the faculty should embrace distance learning as a way for more students to access their courses, resulting in a greater intellectual audience and less chance of a course being cancelled due to low enrolment.

The web profoundly influence society in general and universities in particular. One of the consequences of this tremendous surge in online communication has been the rapid growth of technology-mediated distance learning at the higher education level.

This extraordinary growth of technology-mediated distance learning in higher education has prompted several different agencies to develop principles, guidelines, or benchmarks to ensure quality distance education. The web is a major technological advancement reshaping not only our society but also that of universities worldwide. In the light of this, universities have to capitalise on the web for both teaching and learning, and one progressive development of this is the use of web-based learning in distance education settings. The benchmarks for quality assurance of web-based learning were considered important, and in general the participated institutions strove to incorporate them into their policies, practices and procedures.

At the same time, there were few benchmarks that did not enjoy consensus among the academic members, and in some instances were not even considered mandatory to ensure quality for web-based learning. In order to have an effective quality assurance model for web-based learning, it will need to conduct study on students' perception on this issue, and incorporate the results with the perception of academic staff to form a more complete picture of the whole quality assurance model.

Each quality assurance system needs to be careful in analysing the situation of the specific institution. It needs to be very flexible in its approach, and the combination of process and technology needs to be carefully considered, as unintended consequences in one area can originate from a bad choice in another. It may be worth noting that a firm adherence to an explicit view of what constitutes good web-based learning, and an explicit view of issues of change and culture will furthermore influence the specific approach taken in assuring the quality web-based learning.

For education, broadband access means the elimination of time and distance from the learning equation. Broadband carries with it powerful multimedia learning opportunities, the full interactivity of instructional content, and the quality and speed of communications. Wireless solutions may enable underdeveloped and remote areas to quickly take advantage of the web via wireless phones, two-way pagers, and hand-held devices.

During this period, internet access in households has grown dramatically. In just a year and a half the share of households with internet access doubled, rising from 26.2 per cent to 41.5 per cent. Rural households are catching up. Home access is important for students doing research, taking online courses, and communicating with teachers and other learners. For parents, online access means new kinds of communication with their children's schools, with their children's teachers, and with other parents.

For all households, internet access is another way to connect with their communities and government services. Home access helps to advance economic opportunities: low-income users were the most likely to display using the internet to look for jobs. Those learners without internet access at home rely on schools, libraries, and other public places to provide this access. For many economically disadvantaged and minority group youngsters, a computer at school or in the library after school is the only link to the wide world of the internet. Educational institutions are struggling to provide students with internet access, and great strides have been made in bringing schools, libraries, and postsecondary institutions online.

Post-secondary education institutions are also rapidly expanding student access to the internet. The internet is a double-edged sword for these learners. It can be a gateway to new opportunities, or a barrier that challenges them even further. Web-based learning environments can provide support and challenge through multiple means of:

i) Representation (e.g., a math concept in both text and graphic modes; animated science simulations; poetry read aloud by the author, etc.)
ii) Expression (i.e., use of text; sound; images; video; and combinations of media as vehicles for expressive literacy through writing, illustrating, speaking, video-making, and drawing)
iii) Engagement to attract the easily bored or the easily distracted learner. Designing accessibility into an internet site or a course at the beginning is far less expensive than

> after the fact. Designs that create barriers harm everyone, not just people with disabilities.

Teachers are the key to effective use of web-based tools and applications, but first they must become skilled at using them. It is the teacher, after all, who guides instruction and shapes the instructional context in which the internet and other technologies are used. It is a teacher's skill at this, more than any other factor, that determines the degree to which students learn from their internet experiences.

Teachers must be comfortable with technology, able to apply it appropriately, and conversant with new technological tools, resources, and approaches. If all the pieces are put into place, teachers should find that they are empowered to advance their own professional skills through these tools as well.

While younger teachers may have basic technology skills they realise that they, like their older colleagues, do not know how to apply these skills to teaching. The ability to use technology for non-instructional purposes does not necessarily translate into either the will or the capability to use technology to support student learning. Although they are not technophobes, these new teachers lack a clear conception of effective classroom uses of technology in their subject area.

Professional development is the critical ingredient for effective use of technology in the classroom. Seventy per cent of educators polled regarding technology in instruction put professional development at the top of their list of technology challenges. Professional development is often called 'training', but the term implies much more than just building basic technology skills. It means developing a vision built on the understanding that technology is a tool that can offer solutions to longstanding teaching and learning problems.

Fortunately, the internet is making it possible to connect teachers to each other, giving opportunities for mentoring, collaboration, and formal and informal online learning. Through the internet, teachers have access to high quality online professional development opportunities beyond what the local school or district is able to offer. And, in working in online environments, teachers obtain a collateral benefit: they learn important technological skills.

In short, a supportive social structure is one of the key elements for successful online learning. But unless new teachers enter the classroom ready to teach with technology, students will never catch up with modern technology. If teacher education programmes do not address this issue head on, they lose the opportunity to get it right with a whole generation of new teachers and the students they teach.

WEB-LEARNING ENVIRONMENTS

Today's sophisticated online learning and performance needs, the consideration of a comprehensive set of human factors that contribute to online solutions from a whole-person perspective, are critical. Traditionally, designers have focused on primarily cognitive factors (e.g., how people build, process, and store knowledge). These primarily cognitive designs often overlook other sources for individual learning differences, such as emotions and intentions. If even they are considered, they are often relegated to a secondary role.

Historically, these approaches reflect the industrial-age perspective that assumes that an instructor is available in the classroom and can respond to the audience's diverse range of complex human needs. As a result, instructors have often unintentionally created a learning dependence that detracts from the learner's ability to self-motivate, self-manage, and self-assess online learning. And also suggests that conventional classroom design methodologies and solutions may need enhancement for online learning, and designers need alternative learning models that help learners become more independent, self-motivated, and self-managed online learners.

For online learners, the lack of an instructor is emerging as a problem simply because many learners are not very experienced at self-motivated or self-managed learning. The new learner-difference models should address this problem by:

i) explaining how emotions, attitudes, beliefs, and intentions (in addition to the more commonly recognised cognitive and social factors) and their relationships influence, support, or undermine learning experiences,
ii) considering the impact of these factors and explain how they may influence more successful online learning, and
iii) providing guidelines for designing instruction and learning environments that help learners not only meet instructional objectives, but also improve online learning ability.

Learning orientations are helpful because they describe key attributes of the learning audience, including their proclivity to learn more successfully. There are four learning orientations:

i) transforming,
ii) performing,
iii) conforming; and
iv) resistant.

These profiles provide three specific scales for measuring key learner-difference attributes. Learning orientations have a variety of uses: they help to differentiate the audience for research, guide analysis and design of research, instruction, and environments, tailor solutions that improve performance, learning ability, and online relationships, and making the overall learning experience more satisfying and worthwhile.

One learning environment, was adapted and matched three learning orientations. The purpose was to test what effects the adapted presentations had on the learning experience. The learning orientation model served as a foundation to measure, analyse, and explain the effects and interactions on multiple dependent variables over three time periods. This mass customisation approach highlighted emotions and intentions as a dominant influence on learning.

An instructional research called the System for Intentional Learning and Performance Assessment (SILPA) was used to create the three adapted presentations in one learning environment. The SILPA can presents three different environments that can match the learning orientations, foster improved learning ability, and replace traditional, "one-size-fits-all" solutions. The SILPA can diagnose the audience in advance of the instruction with the electronic version of the Learning Orientation Questionnaire (LOQ). The Intentional Learning Training (ILT) was presented to the learners in the web learning environment. The purpose of this intervention was to provide online learning tools and suggest to learners how they might improve their online ability with tools for more self-directed learning.

These tools enabled learners to manage individual learning performance for the domain of expertise in an organised problem-solving structure integrated with dynamic practice and assessment activities.

By using e-learning techniques as part of a 'blended' learning approach, retail financial services organisations can not only improve customer satisfaction, but also protect their organisations from unwanted risks. This is necessary in today's rapidly changing environment that includes pressures from many different directions:

i) *Regulation*: the increasing burden of regulation creates an environment in which staff must be kept uptodate and requires that their employer can demonstrate compliance.
ii) *Product development*: product lifecycles are becoming shorter and products more complex. The staff need to know new product options and requirements, often at short notice to meet customer demand.
iii) *Risk control and compliance:* ensuring full compliance with both internal and external processes and procedures

and ensuring that the organisation always gives the same advice in response to the same circumstances are necessary,

iv) *Increasing emphasis on sales*: the staff may need to acquire new skills in order to make the transition from transaction processing to customer service and sales.

v) *Mergers and acquisitions*: driving value from a merger or acquisition means that the staff must learn new methods and practices, for example, when the systems from one business are rolled out into the other.

vi) *Open finance alliances*: the staff must learn to sell and service products from a different market sector, for example, the sale of insurance products through a bank branch network.

vii) *High staff turnover:* some areas of the retail financial services industry can suffer from attrition rates of 30 per cent or more.

viii) *Efficiency*: today's market environment has forced a sharp focus on costs.

The most effective learning is achieved through a structured combination of approaches including face-to-face training, online learning and traditional self-study material—this is the essence of blended e-learning. The use of e-learning is flexible, cost effective and less time-consuming than traditional 'chalk and talk' classroom-based training. Yet e-learning will only succeed as part of an integrated strategy that uses the right learning mechanism for a particular subject. Any e-learning system needs to be integrated with other business dimensions and applications. A unique e-learning service is proven to deliver real bottom line results. By combining learning expertise with systems integration and business consulting, Syntegra is able to support all aspects of e-learning, including helping customers to generate appropriate content and monitoring. Syntegra has an extensive track record in training and pioneered the blended e-learning approach.

At the heart of any successful e-learning offering lies a learning management system (LMS). Some of the leading providers of LMS applications worldwide, in particular Syntegra have extensive capabilities with Docent, a product offering that extends beyond its core LMS and has leveraged partnerships for distribution and implementation. Docent systems have been built to scale for hundreds of thousands of users worldwide. Syntegra developed a unique e-learning environment, which offers a combination of an e-learning portal and community site for e-learning professionals.

BENEFITS OF E-LEARNING

The educational system of today needs to impart to all learners three new foundational skills: to make learning a relevant and lifelong process—a process of continuous growth change and evolution and adaptation. The schools of the twentieth century were clustered around the idea that time would be constant and learning would be variable. Today with computers taking over, jobs that can be done with minimum education are fast diminishing.

The idea of schools as a fixed time activity is being replaced by the concept of continuous learning built around a variety of tools and techniques. The twenty-first century classroom will be wherever the learner is located—at school, on the bus ride home, in the park, at a museum, or in the playground. Traditional tools will co-exist with the hitech tools of the telematic era.

The teacher's role in this distributed setting is to be quite different from that of content presenter and test giver. The teacher in this setting will operate in a system based on four components: campfires, watering holes, caves, and life. The campfire is the informational space associated with lectures and other methods of direct instruction. The watering hole is the conversational space occupied when learners converse among themselves or with their teachers about a particular topic. The cave is the conceptual space where ideas are developed in relative solitude and where student projects are designed and built. Life is the contextual space where the things have been learned and are applied in the world outside of school.

Learning has always taken place in these four spaces, yet twentieth century schools often failed to provide the right balance and learning suffered as a result. These four learning spaces provide a framework for the community at large that can envision educational opportunity. Flexibility is the key for the effective definition of the roles. Technology can become the force that equalises the educational opportunities of a children regardless of location and social and economic circumstances.

The internet eliminates geography as a limiting factor. A child in a remote hamlet can have the same access to the same reference materials as one located in the cosmopolitan city. Time is transcended by telematic tools. Technology will have an increasingly positive impact on the student's creativity. Access to multiple expressive modalities is important.

Educators are also great beneficiaries of the telematic revolution. It opens up new opportunities for casual dialogues on a wide range of topics, and helps overcome the sense of isolation sometimes felt by educators whose areas of interest have few local enthusiasts. In addition to conversing with peers, communication with learners, their parents, the community at large is facilitated with the same tools. Though technology promises the panacea to better learning, sales hungry decision makers have exploited it. Now it is faced with the challenge of maintaining the delicate balance between quality and quantity.

Society has been credited with creating technology, but technology is simultaneously creating society. These observations would also suggest that technology is beginning to exercise a benevolent tyranny over humankind. People have become compulsive information consumers who favour the passive reaction of information as a form of entertainment over the more challenging act of thinking.

Maintaining quality presupposes building a code of ethics into the telematic infrastructure, just as science without responsibility is like a sword without a sheath; so too, telematic education without ethics will lead to gross debasement of human energies. The ethical values to bear in mind cannot be isolated from human values and responsibilities. It should also provide built-in evaluative means that protect internal human ecological aspects. Primarily quality checks must respect human rights to privacy, to avoid intrusion and abuse of these rights, and to avoid placing all information on equal levels.

REFERENCES

Davie, L., "Facilitation techniques for the on-line tutor", In *Mindweave: Communications, Computers, and Distance Education*, eds. R. Mason and A. Kaye, 74-85, Oxford: Pergamon Press, 1989.

Harasim, L., "On-line education: A new domain", In *Mindweave: Communications, Computers, and Distance Education*, eds., R. Mason and A. Kaye, 50-62, Oxford: Pergamon Press, 1989.

Knowles, M. S., *The Modern Practice of Adult Education, From Pedagogy to Andragogy*, New York: Cambridge, 1980.

Kristensen, T., "A Pedagogical network of schools in the Bergen region", In TeleTeaching, eds. G. Davies and B. Samways, 523-528, Proceedings of the IFIP TC3 Third Teleteaching Conference, *TeleTeaching* 93, Trondheim, Norway, 20-25 August, 1993.

Paulsen, M.F., *The Online Report on Pedagogical Techniques for Computer-Mediated Communication*, 1995.

4
Web-based Teaching

In schools, the rapid increase in the availability of computers and other technologies has made significant changes in the education system. The teacher's role changes to that of a coach or guide as well as an instructor. Technology creates opportunities for students to work together, such as on group projects in which students exchange ideas about the project and about how to use technology to answer their questions. The focus shifts toward more active student learning. The teacher's skill in using technology is a major factor in improving student learning with technology.

Teachers must know not only how to use technology but also when and why to use it. Teacher technology standards identify essential skills teachers need for effective use of computers and other electronic equipment in schools today. The teacher technology standards or guidelines that address several levels of competency:

i) Fundamental computer operations skills and understanding of technology concepts and terms;

ii) Ability to use technology for personal research and communication;

iii) Understanding of legal and ethical issues pertaining to computer use, such as how copyright applies to classroom software use, and what additional safety measures may be needed in the classroom;

iv) The ability to use computers in a variety of ways to integrate technology into classroom activities that support student learning.

Of these standards, the most difficult one for teachers is the requirement that they know how to integrate technology into instruction. For example, teachers should know what technology is appropriate for use with a particular lesson. At the same time they also must know how to manage the classroom to effectively guide students using the computer.

These standards reflect fundamental concepts and skills for applying information technology in educational settings.

i) *Basic computer/technology operations and concepts*: Candidates will use computer systems to run software; to access, generate and manipulate data; and to publish results. They also will evaluate performance of hardware and software and apply basic troubleshooting strategies as needed.

ii) *Personal and professional use of technology*: Candidates will apply tools for their own professional growth and productivity. They will use technology in communicating, conducting research and solving problems. In addition, they will plan and participate in activities that encourage lifelong learning and will promote equitable, ethical and legal use of computer/technology resources.

iii) *Application of technology in instruction*: Candidates will apply computers and related technologies to support instruction in their grade level and subject areas. They must plan and deliver instructional units that integrate a variety of software, applications and learning tools. Lessons developed must reflect effective grouping and assessment strategies for diverse populations.

If teachers are expected to meet standards of technology competency, quality professional development must be available to help them integrate technology into instruction. Rapid changes in technology are a challenge for schools and states trying to keep teachers uptodate. Another challenge is teachers' lack of access to adequate equipment and software. For example, a teacher who participates in an e-mail training session needs to have the chance to use that new skill upon returning to the classroom. Training without access to equipment is a waste of time and money.

Technology gradually is infused into training. Teachers participate in intensive workshops and contribute lesson plans that incorporate technology into the classroom to share with others in the programme. Teachers also point to the lack of quality training in ways to integrate technology into the teaching process. As educators become more skilled with computer equipment, they need training in applying these skills in the classroom. Professional development in technology until recently has reflected "one size fits all" thinking, and training has focused on broad technical skills rather than specific uses for technology in the classroom.

However, teachers of different grade levels or subjects have different needs for technology training. A first-grade teacher may use a computer to help reinforce students' reading skills. But a high school science teacher needs to use specialised equipment and software to conduct experiments in the classroom and spreadsheets to gather and analyse the data collected.

ONLINE TEACHING TOOLS

The internet provides academics with an opportunity to make their teaching better, to allow them to teach in different ways to the standard one-to-many lecture, and to reach more students. Simply put, it allows for the 'maximisation' of learning. In other words the internet allows for a more efficient and interesting way of 'imparting knowledge'. To add to this, the internet can display the following advantages. In most cases it is:

i) cheap
ii) easy to use
iii) fashionable
iv) attractive to students
v) cross-platform
vi) suitable for accessing resources of various media
vii) ideally suited for remote learning, i.e. 'remote' from the classroom either by location or time
viii) interlinking, providing access to resources held in other subject areas and institutions
ix) suited to increasing collaborative work and cross-institution communication.

Traditionally the internet seemingly provides two options. The first is a form of distance learning in which a tutor places courseware on a web server where it can be accessed by remote students' identifying the disadvantages of such a system as being expensive if one is to insure enough software to meet the demands of a complete syllabus. Alternatively there is the independent study in which learners search the internet for materials that are relevant to their interests. Again this has disadvantages most notably because the suitability of the material students access cannot be guaranteed.

In internet-based Learning (IBL), a learner is provided with access to courseware stored on the campus or the internet from either location. A successful teaching model could involve then orientating, motivating, presenting, clarifying, elaborating, consolidating, and confirming.

Along with lifelong learning, one of the most overused expressions at the moment is that of 'resource-based learning' or 'RBL'. Simply put, this focuses on the concept of giving the learner greater access to resources. Due to the multimedia and easy to access advantages of the internet, the use of online teaching has led many to advocate the policy of marrying the two together.

There is no simple answer to this, as it depends entirely on the teaching goals of the course, and the technological capability of the host institution. As a guide, however, it can be looked on as a straightforward trade-off: increased virtuality means more work required for setting up the course and insuring its success.

WEB-BASED INSTRUCTION

Web-based Instruction (WBI) is a hypermedia-based instructional programme, which utilises the attributes and resources of the World Wide Web to create a meaningful learning environment where learning is fostered and supported. The integral parts of a WBI system such as content development, software, hardware and internet service providers, 'features' the characteristics of a WBI programme contributed by these components. The development of the web coincided with radical changes in patterns of work and the kinds of skill required in the workplace.

A systems analysis to education, regarding the knowledge worker as a 'process component' generating new knowledge which will keep the organisation for which he or she works 'ahead of the competition'. To achieve this, existing knowledge, seen as the input to the system, must be searched and filtered to identify what is relevant to the current task. The accelerated increase in the existing stock of knowledge and its rate of production threaten to swamp the system. The knowledge worker is regarded as responsible for controlling the nature of the new knowledge in a wider social context. The role of the education system is seen as equipping the knowledge worker with the competencies to generate new knowledge responsibly. Four key competencies are identified:

i) *Self-directed and just-in-time learning*: the example of the need to learn how to use new software to perform a task illustrates the need for individual learner-centred access to relevant information at the time of use.

ii) *Self-directed knowledge acquisition*: the knowledge worker needs to be able to access what is relevant from a vast pool of potentially useful information. Hypermedia are seen as a possible solution to structuring this information in accessible forms.

iii) *Information analysis*: it is important to be able to find and critically evaluate the relevant information.

iv) *Creative problem solving*: here recognises the need for synthetic thinking in generating new knowledge by linking existing ideas to each other and the task in new ways.

Such skills are best acquired by experiential learning, for instance the use of case studies and collaborative problem solving activities. There are three computer technologies which could be valuable educational supports:

i) *Electronic performance support systems*: these consist of packages of training and reference materials and specialised software, often distributed across a network by a server. It is suggested that these packages could be delivered over the web.

ii) *Multimedia, hypermedia and the web*: The web offers immediate access to a vast store of information linked by hyperlinks, though its continued expansion depends on capacity to transmit exponentially increasing traffic and availability of access, particularly in less developed countries. To make effective use of the web, information must be organised in a form comprehensible to the user. Improvements in search engines and site design may play a major part in facilitating access.

iii) *Computer mediated communication*: this enables fast but asynchronous collaborative activity. This could enable the experiential learning experiences needed to acquire skills in synthesis and creative problem solving, but make expensive use of skilled educators.

The accessibility of WBI is increasingly finding consumers, including faculty, interested in furnishing educational opportunities through the internet. WBI is a hypermedia-based instructional programme which utilises the attributes and resources of the world wide web to create a meaningful learning environment where learning is fostered and supported. The availability of web-based courses makes higher education attainable.

There are many components and features inherent to WBI, including: interactivity; multimedia capabilities; independence from device, distance, and design; global accessibility; online resources and support; learner control; convenience; ease of use; cost-effectiveness; nondiscriminatory application; and collaborative learning. While many of these features may be attractive to educators, the vast array of capabilities associated with WBI creates the need for consideration of a number of factors prior to the implementation of WBI.

WBI formats generally are divided into in three categories. The first category incorporates text and graphics. This approach requires the use of hypertext markup language (HTML). HTML is the text-based language used to create web pages and hypermedia, linking text and images to additional information. The second category of WBI incorporates interactivity, in which web-based training engages the learner in simulation and provides the learner with immediate results of actions.

Interactive multimedia is the third category of WBI. Multimodal interactivity, including audio and video, are key features within the interactive multimedia category. The interactive multimedia format is becoming more of the standard than ever before because of improved transfer speeds, available storage space, and ease of revision and updating. However, when designing WBI, a needs assessment should be conducted. This needs assessment should be based on learner needs such as experience with the topic, technology, and reason for taking the course.

The internet offers (a) access to potentially unlimited sources, (b) opportunities to develop extensive course content, (c) informal learning processes, and (d) reinforcement of the student's active construction of knowledge. Potential benefits of using the internet include increased enrolment income through the ability to attract students at a distance. Additionally, since students are typically no longer occupying classrooms and university computer systems, there could be a reduced need for infrastructure in equipment and physical plant. The web will be used as a means for delivering instruction despite the absence of a solid research base supporting its effectiveness.

Online learning outcomes such as programme completion, skill acquisition, and student satisfaction have been shown in some instances to be equal or superior to face-to-face (F2F) classroom instruction. However, while both WBI and traditional instruction are effective educational pedagogues, like all instructional methods, they possess both advantages and disadvantages. There are many advantages to using the internet to deliver WBI.

Web-based education prohibits individual students from dominating conversation, potentially drawing out intimidated students who ordinarily choose not to speak up in class. Interactivity is important to enable feedback and support for students. Since the WBI instruction affords both asynchronous and synchronous interchanges many different aspects of instruction may be accomplished.

Web-based instruction prohibits the use of visual cues, which can be used to emphasise specific information and perspectives for student benefit. Further, because of loss of connectivity, students might feel that the educational process is quite removed or fragmented to the degree that they feel they are not learning what they should be learning. WBI includes issues with computer equipment and related interfacing technology. Included is this equipment area are servers that hold the information, the phone lines or hard wires that connect the equipment, the quality of the software that is used to download the information and, finally, the skill of the people using the equipment.

Other weaknesses that affect the quality of learning through the WBI process include rapid changes in technology that require large expenditures to keep up with speed and consumer needs, formatting issues around browser settings and preferences, and variance in browsers being used to access the information. Another area that confounds the issue of successfully using WBI is the continued existence of computer or technological illiteracy and lack of motivation of students/ learners to make use of web-based instruction.

Pedagogy is dictated by the educational philosophy of the instructor. Philosophies may vary, some lending themselves to WBI more than others, but too often content and pedagogy are overlooked, as technology personnel, not educators, lead the drive toward WBI. One approach to the development of web-based content and instruction is supported in the theory behind online learning.

Trends in education, business, and technology mandate that both become lifelong learners; in the process, each becomes both student and teacher. As WBI processes between instructor and student are no longer solely through face-to-face (F2F) contact, communication expectations change, necessitating specification of all modes of support at the beginning of coursework and consideration of both instructor with student expectations.

Communication must be initiated and then maintained by ongoing efforts. Text-based communication, typically the essence of distance education (DE) communication, can be easily misread; therefore, care must be taken to provide clear communications and prevent miscommunications.

Online instruction requires that the student become an active learner, constructing his or her own knowledge from the direction provided by the instructor. WBI can transform passive students into active students, with instructors guiding and facilitating, aiding them in the tasks of analysing and synthesising information. Educators in WBI become more like coaches and facilitators linking students directly to desired resources and sources of information rather than acting in the traditional role of delivering information.

Information competency is defined as the ability to access, retrieve, manipulate, relate, understand, and evaluate information in order to fulfil expected levels of performance (ROI)—awareness, information, application, and systematic integration. The basic characteristics of WBI result in changes in the dynamics of the relationship between instructor and student.

Some of the obvious differences between web-based and campus-based instruction include an increased reliance on technology, the need for advanced development of instructional materials, and a shift in learning responsibilities to the student. Yet the creation of WBI is a time-consuming process, especially when performed thoughtfully and thoroughly to include planning, design, development, delivery, evaluation, and maintenance. Design considerations include determining the specific needs and characteristics of the audience, and establishing the goals and objectives of the course.

The second stage, development, consists of creating a content outline, reviewing existing materials for compatibility with medium and course, organising and developing content to be as integrated as possible, and selecting and developing materials and methods integrating modalities. In the third stage, the evaluation stage, goals and objectives are reviewed, an evaluation plan is developed and decisions are made regarding the use of formative, summative, quantitative, and qualitative evaluation; then data are collected and analysed. Evaluation is conducted on the use of technology, course formats, course atmosphere, quantity and quality of interaction, acquisition of content, assignments, tests, support services, student achievement, student attitude, and instructor.

Costs associated with WBI include:

a) purchase/lease of instructional materials, including software and hardware;
b) equipment maintenance,
c) telecommunication fees—broadcasting, connecting, delivering, and disseminating information;
d) personnel, including full-time faculty, adjunct faculty, graduate and undergraduate assistants, technical personnel, clerical personnel, contracted personnel from other departments, and outside designers and consultants;
e) components of direct costs—planning, course production, course maintenance, mediating/tutoring, and student assessment;
f) delivery of the instruction and associated costs; and
g) time and money for training faculty and staff in the use of hardware and software.

WBI potentially offers several cost benefits:

i) a smaller number of faculty can reach a larger number of students;
ii) expenses for physical building space and operational costs such as air conditioning, electricity, water, etc., may be reduced; and
iii) students carry the financial responsibility of accessing the hardware and software necessary to complete course requirements.

The costs of WBI, however, cannot always be addressed in terms of a return on investment. WBI requires physical space only for the server, the development hardware, and, possibly, for software storage. A computer laboratory housing hardware and software for production may already exist within the department or university, thus providing the needed physical space for development of instruction and materials. Planning for WBI includes determining the location of the instruction. Instruction can be stored on a university server, a department server, the instructor's server, or on a server belonging to a partner organisation.

Increased capabilities in software can result in greater quality and efficiency, but also require more random access memory (RAM) and hard drive space for materials produced. Not all users will be accessing the course with computers whose specifications match those of the development machine or server, so state-of-the-art equipment may not be appropriate. The more technology incorporated into the design, the less accessible the instruction becomes to the majority; therefore, students should be provided with high calibre instruction even if using a slower speed computer and modem. It is critical that WBI incorporate accessibility for individuals with disabilities. User-friendly web page development software can be purchased to create websites, although knowledge of HTML is helpful for editing purposes.

Software can be used to create, alter, and animate images, as well as to create full motion video and high quality sound. Authoring software also provides opportunities to incorporate interactive multimedia components, and additional utilities can aid in creating searchable, web-accessible document files. However, if the course will include audio and/or video, several factors must be considered: the quality of the media and its potential download speeds, the worthiness of including such media, the possible necessity for the download of plug-ins for accessibility, and the source of plug-ins should the user require them.

Interactive Learning

Interactivity is one of the attractive components of web-based education and is not limited to the use of hypertext and the media. When talking about interactivity, we should refer not so much to interaction with learning material that someone has made available on the network or on CD-ROM, but rather to human-machine interaction governed by software, or, better still, personal interaction mediated by network technology.

Even when using the technology's potential to the fullest, there is no guarantee about the quality that interaction will bring to the learning process. The development of new technology, especially over the past decade, has led to the production of multimedia material of high quality, at least in aesthetic terms. Looking at these products from the communication viewpoint, we can identify two extremes. At one end, there are products with a low level of interactivity, which tend to reproduce the traditional lecture format.

Another type of interactivity, is direct interactivity between individuals, where the technology does not "drive" but acts as a passive mediator. This is the case with computer networks. While interactivity is no guarantee of quality, social interaction with peers or with one's trainers plays a key role in the learning process, both from the psychosocial and psycho-affective viewpoints. In this sense, ICT services can make an enormous contribution. Despite this, there is still a general trend in distance education toward one-way schemes.

Interaction is imperative if the quality of the process is to be raised: interaction with materials, between students and their tutors/teachers, as well as between all the participants. Information technology and, more importantly, computer communication technology can play a vital role in fostering this interaction, even if use of these means is not in itself a guarantee of higher quality. As is usually the case, a fundamental role is played by course designers and coordinators, who have the means to steer the process toward the predefined goals.

However, raising interactivity in the process either involves investing in multimedia products which are very complex and expensive, or entails increasing the amount of online tutoring. Courseware tools also have been developed over the past few years to aid in the development of electronic learning environments by integrating access to information, interactivity, and synchronous and asynchronous communication.

Human infrastructure is the foundation of student learning, and physical, technological, and human elements must be integrated. Human infrastructure is critical to total institutional infrastructure; technology is impacting not only physical infrastructure but human infrastructure as well. As new teaching-learning paradigms evolve, the faculty must be strengthened through training and university supports. Investment in the development of faculty will build the human infrastructure essential to technology-driven higher education.

The web is not an interactive tool unless elements are incorporated to promote that interaction. The development of WBI, however, requires an even higher level of understanding. Engaging in WBI requires not only the instructor or developer to have a level of expertise in WBI but the student as well. Both must possess a level of knowledge or aptitude enabling them to perform the basic operations of both the computer hardware and system software. Both must be able to apply simple problem solving techniques as well as have a general understanding or foundation in how to navigate the WWW and use functions such as e-mail and/or fax.

The remote student in WBI will also need access to the same student services as on-campus students, such as registration, tuition payment, student support, examinations, and library services. Creating WBI without marketing and promoting the availability of course work deflates the potential profitability that increased enrolment can offer. It also prevents meeting the identified need. If the department or university does not have an individual or group of individuals designated to promote web-based courses, marketing efforts will become a faculty responsibility.

The development of an online syllabus and readings could be the entrance into WBI, followed by the incorporation of hyperlinks and the addition of text and image-based instructional materials. Professors are currently creating web pages for courses, syllabi, readings, and links. E-mail may initially serve as the primary mode of communication, followed by the incorporation of a listserv, then synchronous chats.

WEB-BASED EDUCATION: PROBLEMS AND PROSPECTS

There is a dominance of web-courses in the fields of computer and information sciences and by courses in education. Except from these two fields, web courses cover a very broad range of subjects. The number of subject areas that was offered varied considerably between the institutions. Nearly half of the institutions offer courses in only one category and only five offered courses in five or more categories. An administrative system should be able to handle students, teachers, courses, and course material.

An online college may have to handle thousands of students, hundreds of teachers, and a large number of courses with password restricted web pages, discussion forums, distribution lists, class rosters, and student presentations. It may also have to provide administrative systems for the dispatch of textbooks, handling of tuition and examination fees, and organisation of local examinations. These services constitute a major challenge for many traditional institutions. Institutions that plan to offer large scale and professional online education need an administrative system, which is integrated with the web.

The simplest strategy is probably to collaborate with an institution that already has a functional administrative system. Another solution, which requires more technical competence, is to develop an in-house system based on common internet services. The online education for standard systems are continuously being improved, but they may still need much local adaptation. They may only meet some of the administrative needs, and they could place some pedagogical limitations on the courses.

Many of the institutions have developed in-house administrative solutions in combinations with standard internet software. The tuition fees for web courses seem to vary considerably among institutions and courses. Some courses are free and open to everyone, and others seem to have full or partial external funding. The institutions that operate with tuition fees seem to have fees that are the same or not very different from fees in traditional courses.

The analysis has revealed few, if any, examples of institutions with substantial income from student fees. Likewise, there seem to be few institutions that can claim that provision of web-based courses has been an economic success, if they disregard external research and development grants.

The tutors seem to be both part-time teachers that are engaged just for the online courses and full-time teachers that also teach some online courses. It is also interesting to observe that distributed experts and students take part in the tutoring. Human tutoring seems to be much more common than machine tutoring, but some institutions include machine tutoring in addition to human tutoring.

Most institutions seem to combine individual tutoring with group tutoring. The focus between the two could however vary. Online teaching is in many courses supplemented with face-to-face meetings, video- or audio-conferences, or telephone contact.

There are a number of barriers that must be overcome before online education can become a large-scale success. Among them are financial barriers, resistance to change, bandwidth limitations, access limitations, insufficient search facilities, copyright issues, and barriers to online assessment.

The financial barriers are important. The analysis showed that few institutions had substantial income from student fees. At the same time, the cost of development and maintenance could be high. In addition, national regulations in some countries deny institutions the opportunity to charge tuition fees.

REFERENCES

Galusha, J. M., *Barriers to Learning in Distance Education, Interpersonal Computing and Technology*, 5(3-4), pp. 6-14, 1998.

Harasim, L., "On-line education: A new domain", In *Mindweave: Communications, Computers, and Distance Education*, eds. R. Masonand A. Kaye, 50-62. Oxford: Pergamon Press, 1989.

Johnson, E., "Teaching on international computer networks", *TEXT Technology* 3(2):3-5, 1993.

5
Interface Design in Computer Mediated Classes

Interface design is an important factor in determining how well a human can interact with a computer system. However, the issue of ethics in interface design seems to receive considerably less attention. Historically off-line processing and trained operators provided an environment where the lack of ethics in design did not cause major problems. The environment of humans interacting with computers is changing rapidly and ethics should become increasingly important.

Current interface design most often requires an interface that allows immediate interaction and feedback. The design of the interface can introduce bias and this in turn can disadvantage or offend users because of gender, age, culture and the workplace environment. The historical background of human computer interaction and the increasing relevance of ethical considerations at the interface, global communication and interaction with its many cultures and conflicting norms highlight the need for a strong ethical foundation in interface design.

Learners must be empowered through thoughtful interaction to acquire the necessary skills to effectively work in an open-ended environment. Distance education places fewer restrictions on learners, and learners must take greater responsibility for their educational experiences. Frequently, learners are under major time constraints with work and family obligations, and being efficient with their graduate studies is an important issue.

Teachers realise that computer-mediated education requires developing a new contemporary vision of learning. These new teaching strategies will demand changing the traditional role of teachers from information transmitters. The term education describes a teaching and learning concept that transcends just merely sharing factual information. It assumes that a capable teacher will know where he or she is going. The wise teacher seeks to guide his students toward greater maturity, preparing them to effectively adapt to a rapidly changing world. As educators refine their philosophy of distance learning, they are concerned about sustaining interactivity in their educational process.

Today's adult learning theories are built upon the premise that teachers will assist their students to become self-directed and independent. Learners must assume responsibility for their educational experiences, but independent study has natural limitations. If learners do not receive adequate teacher feedback and reinforcement, students will not always know whether they possess an accurate knowledge of their subject matter.

Teachers are still considered knowledge experts who have a clear understanding of their subject matter. Yet, their new role involves promoting more self-directed learning activities that cultivate achieving knowledge objectives through personal study. Teachers are challenged to carefully design instructional activities that guide their students into online learning situations that promote personal acquisition of knowledge.

Teachers strive to encourage positive learning habits that foster both self-directed learning styles and genuine collaboration with other classmates. It requires planning creative online instructional assignments that intellectually stretch their students but does not confuse or overwhelm them.

For instance, teachers should not consider sharing a lecture transcript unless there were specific questions and class discussion that supported the reading of their lecture material.

Distance educators view computer-mediated education as an excellent format to encourage a variety of adult learning styles while serving an ethnically diverse student population. Genuine interactivity (communication, participation and feedback) should empower learners to cultivate both self-directed instructional skills and develop enriching dialogue with other students.

The issue of interactivity is a vital issue for teachers as they seek to create classwork that promotes lively academic dialogue and cultivates critical thinking skills. A major problem involved students not receiving adequate feedback from their teachers. In fact, today's distance educators are developing a new set of terms to describe the learning problems in virtual classes. The word cyberia refers to "a place to which online students feel they have been regulated when they receive no feedback from their instructor."

The syllabus plays a vital role in helping students understand the teacher's expectations and establishes a foundation for positive learning experiences. The syllabus does help bring structure and sets the tone to the online educational setting.

Teachers give students instructional influence based on factors such as their knowledge of the subject matter and the type of learning assignment. Computer-mediated education is self-paced and learners are given various opportunities to create relevant and interesting work. The distance education format challenges teachers to develop a learning environment that places more responsibility on the student to accomplish academic tasks with minimal teacher assistance.

Teachers appreciate the lively debates that characterise most online classes. Frequently, learners offer thought-provoking dialogues because they have time to reflect on the posted comments before sharing their thoughts. Educators need to be creative in moderating online discussions because every class contains a unique set of individuals who respond differently to the operating in the online environment.

The teaching and learning process is dynamic and somewhat fluid. If educators are serious about promoting self-directed learning, then their assessment philosophy should reinforce the importance of giving students opportunities to influence evaluation. A comprehensive picture of evaluation must include student perceptions because they can provide insights into individual testing instruments, term papers, and online class discussions.

Learner observations are valuable for gaining a good perspective on the total educational experience. Educators can use a variety of evaluation formats that offer opportunities to improve the teaching and learning process. Instructors can use telephone calls and e-mail messages to individual learners as excellent ways to cultivate informal feedback that can be used to make immediate course changes.

Educators need to take a fresh look at instructional procedures that help them "approach non-traditional problems in non-traditional ways". Unfortunately, some educators are complacent about their professional growth or resist making instructional changes. Yet, teachers do have a professional responsibility to implement innovative assessment techniques into their teaching practices.

Teachers must develop dialogues with their students that foster personal and professional growth. Unfortunately, some professors, through attitude and verbal and written comments, treat their students as subordinates. Teachers are challenged by the task of evaluating online learner responses that are personally relevant and affirm course learning objectives. Educators must integrate social interaction during their class actives that affirms active participation and self-directed learning.

Contemporary educators are sometimes concerned that distance education is a poor substitute for the traditional classroom. Teachers must consistently affirm the independence and autonomy of their learners by enabling them to freely pursue authentic learning objectives. Yet, the idea of independence does not mean being totally separate or isolated from other learners and teachers. Rather, a balanced perspective would highlight giving learners the power to assume greater responsibility for their educational experiences while actively working with the teacher and other students.

Therefore, the context of learning critical thinking skills is interactive and built upon taking individual responsibility for academic achievements. Genuine reflective thinking requires being dedicated to improving individual academic performance by continuously enhancing cognitive skills. Unfortunately, the concept of critical thinking has been confused with being something quite abstract from daily living. Critical thinking is emotive as well as rational. Critical thinkers tend to look beyond the surface of situations by exploring alternative perspectives.

The advent of the web and its phenomenal growth has similarly reduced the training overhead for accessing course content. Web-based conferencing systems and the support for audio and video on the web complete the current picture of an integrated environment for delivering course content and participant interaction and support through one logon sequence. Web-in-a-box software now takes this environment and packages it for the coalface educator who does not want to be bothered with HTML and needs simple administrative and assessment facilities for tracking student progress.

Many of the early online teachers were dazzled by the new opportunity of group communication with students at a distance. Since unlimited, interactive, time-independent discussion was technically possible, both students and tutors expected it would happen. The fact that educationally beneficial, dynamic and all-inclusive discussions are far from commonplace events in face-to-face teaching, should have prevented the growth of this unreal expectation for the online environment, which almost all early adopters experienced.

While the technology tends to support a certain degree of egalitarian participation, and does allow users the freedom to input messages at their convenience, the conditions which are needed to produce good educational discussions are far more complex, more people-dependent and more educationally determined than mere technology will ever influence very significantly. Most online educators have realised that generating good discussions online takes careful planning and structuring.

The web often acts as the resource around which the activities are designed, in some cases using course-specific materials and readings provided by the tutor, and in other cases using the vast materials from other websites worldwide. Students are often asked to construct a group website as the focus for their joint work. Alternatively they could be asked to work through problems, experiments or simulations presented online and to compare their solutions. Whereas early collaborative activities were largely restricted to discursive areas of the curriculum or to joint writing assignments, the web with its multimedia capabilities has now extended the potential for collaborative work into the image-dependent subjects like science, technology and mathematics.

Technology is rarely the problem—and equally rarely the solution! Sharing computer-based teaching material amongst consortia or on a commercial basis, is the holy grail—much talked of and aspired to even in funded programmes, but so difficult to achieve. The web and to some extent CD-ROMs overcome the early interoperability problems in sharing computer-based software, and quality of teaching material is now the major stumbling block. Many computer-based teaching programmes whether stand alone, on an intranet or the web, fall into one of two categories: all glitz and no substance, or content which reflects a rote-learning, right/wrong approach to learning.

The lifelong learning movement with its emphasis on just-in-time learning and a customer-centred approach has helped to develop the interest in online courses using a resource-based model. The underlying aim of such courses is learning how to learn; that is, facilitating knowledge management skills such as searching, selecting and synthesising information, discovering how and where to find answers and solutions, and understanding, transforming and presenting ideas.

In higher education, current approaches to teaching and learning are dominated by the following: the importance of interactivity in the learning process, the changing role of the teacher from sage to guide, the need for knowledge management skills and for team working abilities, and the move towards resource-based rather than packaged learning. All of these elements figure strongly in the literature of online educators.

Students are more active participants in the online class. Students cannot assume the passive role of simply attending lectures to acquire information. Students are put in a position of being responsible for their learning. They must assume an active role in the learning process to succeed in an online class. Many students are surprised to find that learning is a complicated, ongoing activity that requires input of their time outside of class! An online class has the potential for improving communication among students and between students and faculty.

Students have more opportunities to ask one-to-one questions through e-mail and chat sessions. Students are less inhibited by the keyboard and monitor than they are by a room full of other students. There is a friendly anonymity around a student who is working at a CPU. In an online class, students should be presented with well-edited course materials. If the course lectures are online, students will have error-free lecture notes because they do not have to play stenographer and can download printed copies instead.

An online class is a good way to demonstrate departmental interest/concern for non-traditional students. The student population is extremely diverse, and there are many students who cannot afford to give up their jobs to attend a traditionally scheduled class. These students are often extremely capable and can flourish if given the opportunity to participate in an online class. The students get a message that the department cares about them.

The online class can be offered jointly, giving an enrolment that makes the class financially viable. An asynchronous online class shared between departments or colleges offers scheduling flexibility. This again benefits both departments and students. Class hour conflicts are eliminated. When different instructors teach a class, the online class can improve the consistency of course content from instructor to instructor and from one term to another provided they use the same course web site. Deciding to put a class online also forces someone in the department to review the content and purpose of the course. There is one final benefit to an online class.

The heritage of interactive design for network-based solutions has helped interface designers understand how to apply their craft to create effective World Wide Web solutions. Interface designers can help improve the productivity of information workers, decrease the need for training, and reduce user errors. The web is a revolution in computing, allowing unknown individuals across the world to publish and be heard on the internet. The desktop publishing revolution in the 1980s did not signal an end to professional design, it only flooded the market with poor quality documents.

The web is doing the same for information access by making it possible for anyone to design a web page. However, there is little to help individuals design a web page well, not to mention the problem of sifting through all the useless data that results from searching the web. Interface design concerns how effectively users complete tasks and how well they enjoy their work.

While graphics design focuses on the aesthetics of the interface, together these fields make traditional graphical user interface (GUI) design a strong, but incomplete, foundation for good web design. Not all GUI principles apply, but a majority can help any designer.

Instant feedback and the concept of selection-activation in GUI design are critical to the users interaction with the system. With the HTML form-based menu nothing happens, since you still need to "submit" the request using the View button—an unnatural sequence for users of desktop GUI applications. The submission of an HTML request is similar to sending in a batch of cards in old card readers—you have to wait for a response. This means that all error checking, field validation, and field completion have to occur after submission. In fact, a pop-down menu might be the wrong GUI object to place on the web page. A pop-down menu is best applied to cases where one option is possible from a list of 12 or fewer mutually exclusive items. The pop-down menu does not require as much screen real estate as an imagemap or text list.

Typical GUI objects like buttons, checkboxes, lists, menus, and text fields are available, but without a knowledge of user interface design loss in productivity, increased errors, and inaccurate results are probable if inappropriate objects are used. Understanding the users intention, the context of use and usability testing can accurately reveal the selection of an appropriate HTML object. An alternative to pop-down menus or HTML menus are imagemaps. Poorly designed imagemaps can cause users to spend minutes navigating down the wrong path. This is especially true when accessing a web page via a slow modem line. The difference between a good and bad imagemap can easily come down to its "look and feel". Just because a design looks good does not mean it is functional.

Java allows for user interactions to affect the system in real-time, thus bringing web interaction more in line with traditional desktop GUI software design. There is rhyme and reason in designing for the web. The web gives designers the opportunity to reengineer the front-end of the legacy application. Thus, data can be accessed and viewed using newer more effective presentation methods.

The web is not so radical that traditional concepts of design should be ignored, but knowing how to design for the web is different than for other media. Solid design and usability are features explicity used to sell products to consumers. A user-friendly web interface can have many advantages over an existing legacy interface. These advantages include:

i) Reduced errors due to a redesigned process flows, increased error handling, and embedded help
ii) Increased number of transactions per worker
iii) Increased user acceptance of the system
iv) Reduced strain on users (less mental fatigue and frustration)
v) Increased flexibility for changes and improvements to the system (modular design)
vi) Increased number of platforms supported with a consistent interface across platforms
vii) Worldwide access

Professional analysts and designers generally agree that well-designed user interfaces improve the performance and appeal of the web, helping to convert "tourists" or "browsers" to "residents" and "customers". The user-interface development process focuses attention on understanding users and acknowledging demographic diversity.

But in a global economy, these differences may reflect worldwide cultures. In most projects, the complex interplay of user, business, marketing, and engineering requirements needs to be resolved by web user-interface and information visualisation designers. Their development process includes iterative steps of planning, research, analysis, design, evaluation, documentation, and training. As they carry out all of these tasks, however, they would do well to consider their own cultural orientation and to understand the preferred structures and processes of other cultures.

This attention would help them to achieve more desirable global solutions or to determine to what extent localised, customised designs might be better than international or universal ones. Cultures, even within some countries, are very different. These differences go deeper than mere appearance; they reflect strong cultural values.

REFERENCES

Bellcore, "Guide for Multiplatform Graphical User Interfaces", LP-R13, Issue 2, December 1994.

Horton, W., *The Icon Book: Visual Symbols for Computer Systems and Documentation*, NY, NY: John Wiley and Sons, Inc., 1994.

Laurel, B., Ed., *The Art of Human-Computer Interface Design*, NY, NY: Addison-Wesley, 1990.

Microsoft Corporation, "Windows Interface Guidelines for Software Design", *The Microsoft Guidelines for designing a user interface for Windows-based applications*, Redmond, Washington: Microsoft Press, 1995.

Mullet, K., and D. Sano, "Designing Visual Interfaces - Communication Oriented Techniques", Englewood Cliffs, NJ: Prentice Hall, 1995.

Nielsen, J., E. M. D., Galdo, R. C. Sprung, and P. N. Sukaviriya, "Designing for International Use", *In Proceedings of ACM CHI '90 Conference on Human Factors in Computing Systems*, 1990.

Salasoo, A, E., White, T. Dayton, B. Burkhart, and R. Root, "Bellcore's User Centered Design Approach", In M. Wilkind Ed., Usability in Practice, Boston: Academic Press, 1994.

Tufte, E. R., *The Visual Display of Quantitative Information*, Cheshire, Conn: Graphics Press, 1983.

Virzi, R. A., "Streamlining the Design Process: Running Fewer Subjects", *Proceedings of the Human Factors Society 34th Annual Meeting* (pp. 291-294), Santa Monica, CA: Human Factors Society, 1990.

6

Resource Support in Hitech Learning

Internet is beginning to make learning of all kinds, at all levels, any time, any place, any place a practical reality for every man, woman, and child. But millions still cannot access the internet and do not understand how to use it to harness the global web of knowledge. They do not know how to deal in information, the basic currency of the knowledge economy. They do not know how to find information, how to handle it, how to trade in it, how to invest it for their futures. The individuals, already at risk, will become increasingly marginal in the emerging knowledge economy, unless we change the current, law, the current regulations, and current practices.

The World Wide Web is a tool that empowers society to school the illiterate, bring job training to the unskilled, open a universe of wondrous images and knowledge to all students, and enrich the understanding of the lifelong learner. Web-based education is just beginning, with something of far greater promise emerging in the middle distance. Yet technology, even in its current stage of development, can already allow to realistically dream of achieving age-old goals in education.

In US, the congressional Web-based Education Commission set out to discover how the internet is being used to enhance learning opportunity, and to identify ways that Congress and the President can help local schools, state education agencies, and post-secondary institutions overcome barriers. The work began with face-to-face hearings across America and in virtual hearings on the web. The Commission listened to hundreds of people eager to show how the internet and learning are coming together to meet the needs of their communities and schools.

Web is a medium that today's kids expect to use for expression and communication—the world into which they were born. They also learned that the most important ingredient is not money. It is the presence of a local hero or heroes with the vision, courage, and stamina to challenge the *status quo*. Without this ingredient, more money will be of little benefit.

The interactivity of this new technology makes it different from anything that before. It elicits participation, not passive interest gives learners a place for communication, not isolation. It is not a new form of television. It is the beginning of a new way of learning. In one sense, however, those who urge education to hold back have nothing to worry about. A *de facto* moratorium already exists in most American schools. On average, US firms spend between $3,500 and $5,500 per worker in technology and technological support each year, compared to per student spending on technology that rarely exceeds a couple hundred dollars in the best of circumstances.

Today's education is built on an agrarian model that worked in the years when we were a nation of farmers, foresters, and fishermen. Schooling changed to take on elements of the industrial revolution that worked for the needs of the Industrial Age. New designs are needed to create the "knowledge workers" who will define the Information Age. The market is there. Business is poised to support education with powerful internet solutions.

If this era of globalisation has proven anything, it is that a growing world economy can create a strong and lasting demand for skilled knowledge workers and a technologically savvy workforce. But we have not made the connection to education. We must seize the opportunities and complete these connections—technological and human. And we must advance with constant assessment and reflection. There is still much about learning and the impact of technology we do not know.

To make the most of learning with the internet, we will have to address serious issues. Many of these issues are not new. They have been facing education for decades, and some are reaching a crisis point. The effective use of the internet in education is meaningless without understanding the parts of the system that are already strained: teacher shortages and the need for better preparation and retraining; teacher compensation and the need to provide a more professional work environment; inequalities in school funding; aging school buildings; and poor student performance. These strains are slowing the full deployment of the web for learning.

Kids need information literacy. They expect content to be as exciting as their latest video game. Information can be structured in new ways to support effective searching, use, and understanding. In short, the internet is not a panacea for every problem in education.

The internet is a tool that can help to empower every student and elevate each individual to new levels of intellectual capacity and skill. That is the great opportunity of this new technology. Such a promise is easily made. It will take a greater commitment to keep. Education and training is the second largest sector of the US economy. The education market currently represents approximately 9 per cent of the gross domestic product.

In US, the K-12 e-learning market is estimated at $1.3 billion and is expected to grow to $6.9 billion in 2003. The post-secondary online market is estimated at $1.2 billion and it is expected to grow to $7 billion by 2003. The US corporate e-learning market is estimated at $1.1 billion and it is expected to grow to $11.4 billion by 2003.

The global market for e-learning is estimated at $300 billion and is expected to grow to $365 billion by 2003. Venture capital funding in knowledge enterprises amounted to over $3 billion since January 1999 or about triple the total invested in the previous nine years. Skilled jobs now represent 85 per cent of all jobs, in contrast to 20% in 1950. Between 1998 and 2008 more than two per cent million new skilled information technology (IT) workers will be needed to fill newly created jobs and to replace workers leaving the field. In 1999 nearly 720,000 IT positions went unfilled.

The escalating demand for skilled workers in information technology has led to a lifting of the number of visas for hitech workers from 115,000 to 195,000. The demand for hitech labour in Silicon Valley alone is fully one-third greater than the current hitech workforce nationwide. It is estimated that 50 per cent of all employees' skills become outdated within three to five years. To deal with this, corporate training budgets have increased 23.5 per cent between 1994 and 1999.

Classroom use in corporate training is expected to drop from the current level of 78 per cent to 64 per cent by 2001. The market for web-based corporate learning is expected to reach $11.4 billion by 2003, up from $550 million in 1998. In the last 13 years the number of companies that have opened corporate universities grew from 400 to 1,800. At the current rate the number of corporate universities will exceed the number of traditional universities by the year 2010.

During the twenty-first century US army needs soldiers educated for hitech warfighting and other vital missions. The army also needs help recruiting and retaining soldiers who are eager to learn new skills and earn a degree. Until now, however, the army has had difficulty delivering high levels of quality education to soldiers stationed around the world. Many soldiers take university-based courses while serving, but the costs tend to be high and scheduling difficult. And soldiers rotate locations—a collection of courses from several different institutions may make for a well trained soldier, but may not add up to a full-fledged degree.

The army is responding by launching a major initiative to educate soldiers through a programme called the Army University Access Online 1—a $600 million effort based on laptops and "anywhere, anytime" learning principles. It will help recruiting. It will improve learner retention. And it will help produce the educated, information age soldiers America needs to succeed in the missions and battlefields of tomorrow. The army expects to build the largest online educational portal in the world with the objective of enabling any enlisted army personnel to earn a post-secondary degree or technical certification.

To help in this effort, soldier-students will receive tuition assistance, textbooks, laptops, help-desk support, internet access, academic counselling, extensive course selection, and a command climate that encourages lifelong learning. The army anticipates that within the first three months of the programme 15,000 to 20,000 soldiers will be enrolled and pursuing degrees or professional credentials. The vision for army university is that eventually every one of the army's one million soldiers will be able to take advantage of the programme.

The US army's commitment to distance learning is expected to expand the market for online content and courses, creating incentives for development. This should, in turn, create a much richer set of offerings for online learners in the civilian sector as well. The army's commitment to distance learning is expected to expand the market for online content and courses, creating incentives for development with their service. They will return to civilian life with strong educational credentials and a valuable set of marketable workforce skills.

The web-based learning could transform the academic opportunities and broaden horizons for her students. The high school students needed to go beyond the basic skills approach and transition to the self-directed learning activities they would need later in life. The learning approach offered by NETSchools gives every student and teacher a laptop connected to a Local Area Network through infrared ports installed in each room.

Agricultural students use their laptops to operate the school's commercial greenhouse, enter data in the field, and follow research on plant and animal diseases. After only six months, 80 per cent of hundred high students were accessing the internet daily. Over the course of that first year the 144 students at hundred high scored higher and ranked above the national mean in every subject, as well as total basic skills, on the Stanford Achievement Test (SAT).

RESOURCES OF ONLINE LEARNING

The online resources are more or less judiciously provided to support the educational process. The online resources available could be internal—provided by the institution, or external—made available from other institutions. Millions of individual experts and thousands of online interest groups are reachable via external CMC networks. These constitute a tremendous resource for lifelong learning. Individual experts can be consulted and interviewed via e-mail. An online interest group (OIG) is a group of people with a common interest who convene via CMC. There are thousands of OIGs that can be accessed via international CMC networks and it can be argued that they all have some sort of educational purpose.

The electronic journals are available through external CMC networks. World Wide Web documents, catalogues, and search engines are growing rapidly in numbers. Online information probably cover most of the subjects that are taught in online courses. Online database are organised collections of data that can be accessed via CMC. Utilising these external resources, a course provider could maintain local databases or information services of relevance to the courses. An easier solution could, though, be to provide links to external web services or access to international databases.

Online journals are periodicals that are distributed via CMC networks. They are increasingly important resources for information and learning. Local bulletin boards could be used to redistribute online journals as well as other local information. An enormous number of software applications are available via external and internal CMC networks. Online applications are software programmes that can be executed on a remote computer via a computer network. They include a range of applications from software development tools; via specific applications for statistics, economical analysis, etc., to computer-aided instruction applications. Java applications, that allow users to run remote software applications via their web-browser, gain popularity and have an interesting educational potential.

A software library allows remote users to download software applications from a host computer so that they later can execute the programmes on local microcomputers. Such files are available from a number of host computers. Internet provides a standardised file transfer protocol (FTP) for this purpose and a large number of PC-based bulletin board systems have software exchange as their main service

Since social communication is an essential component of educational activity, online educational environments should provide opportunities for informal discourse. An online cafe can contribute to a sense of community among the users, forging a social bond that may offer motivational and cognitive benefits. Additional online resources for educational use include international networks, databases, library catalogues, and information pools. To benefit the curriculum, these resources could be an integral part of the online activities.

Distance teaching systems need to increase the efficiency of distributing and updating information to students, faculty, and staff. In most distance teaching systems, submission of assignments for correction, evaluation, and feedback is important. Computer scored tests can also be included in online systems, as a substitute for traditional off-line computer scoring. In higher level education, two-way communication by e-mail may be used in the guidance of individual student projects. Many distance education programmes include occasional face-to-face meetings between tutors and students. Sometimes, face-to-face meetings develop into one-way presentation of subject matter.

Electronic classroom discussions can develop into exciting experiences of group learning. In the same vein, the medium seems to foster equality of status between the participants. Finally, special group-learning techniques—such as group submission of assignments, group-learning and presentations, seminars, and project work—may be applied. Most distance education systems are designed for individual learning, but communication between one tutor and a number of individual learners is time consuming.

In an online classroom model, there are three common features. First, the group size is comparable to that in a face-to-face class. Second, there is at least one person responsible for guiding the group's activities and, third, computer conferencing represents the principal mode of communication. Varieties of online classrooms depend on the age of student groups, the educational levels, and the roles taken by the people responsible for the groups. The online game or simulation is a variety of the online classroom which merits further development, since it can build on computer processing in addition to computer conferencing.

Since the combination of CMC and word processors essentially has a textual nature, it has attracted interest within the field of the teaching of writing and language skills. E-mail can provide more regular and faster communication between students and tutors. The education utility is a set of online resources that students and faculty can access. A pedagogical technique is a manner of accomplishing teaching objectives. The techniques are organised according to the four communication paradigms used in computer-mediated communication. The paradigms are information retrieval, electronic mail, bulletin boards, and computer conferencing.

Teachers can employ techniques that utilise these resources via CMC. The techniques could be more or less structured, but they all require minimal interactive participation by the teacher.

The primary use of CMC was to support peer communication and professional development, and to enhance curriculum-based classroom activities. Online databases are organised collections of data that can be accessed via CMC. At the sametime online journals are periodicals that are distributed to subscribers via CMC networks. They are increasingly important resources for information and learning.

Online applications are software programmes that can be executed on a remote computer via a computer network. The online applications include a range of applications from software development tools, via specific applications for statistics, economical analysis, and so on, to computer-aided instruction (CAI) applications.

Students may download application programmes from remote software libraries so that they later can execute the programmes on local microcomputers. Such application programmes are available from a number of host computers. Internet provides a standardised file transfer protocol (FTP) to gain copies of software applications, and a large number of the popular PC-based bulletin board systems have software exchange as their main activity. One way to apply such resources in education is to provide online software libraries with relevant educational software for the students. An online interest group (OIG) is a group of people with a common interest who convene via CMC. There are thousands of OIGs that can be accessed via international CMC networks, and it can be argued that they all have some sort of educational use.

The purpose of these OIGs was to facilitate communication among researchers who wanted to share and compare findings about education and to communicate with consumers of research in education. The mission of the CMC system was to empower rural residents through the sharing of knowledge access skills among rural teachers. These accounts show that access to OIGs obviously have been of value to students in teacher education programmes.

The one-to-one techniques are characterised by a one-to-one relationship and by individualised teaching and learning. The teaching and learning are facilitated in the communication process. So, computer-mediated communication can be an effective support for these techniques when the communication can be conveyed by written text. On the other hand, one may contend that some of these techniques depend so much on personal relationships that frequent face-to-face meetings may be necessary. A learning contract is a technique that can be used to individualise the learning process. Internship is a technique allowing students to practise a future profession under the guidance and supervision of qualified professionals.

Comparing face-to-face teaching and e-mail, e-mail appeared to produce more effective and expanded feedback for students, fuller exploitation of the principles of process writing, and greater satisfaction for teachers and students. The computer mediated communications actually used in the face-to-face game environment usually do not reflect the real world.

The computer can act as the game controller, scheduling the events to occur and providing the outcomes based on the actions the role players take. Due to this, the game can be played in a regulated time manner or in real time. There are many games where playing in real time rather than accelerated time would be beneficial to enhancing the realism, including some of the disaster type games designed to educate people on how to deal with crisis situations.

The CMC-based teaching system has six dimensions. Each dimension was regarded as continuous rather than dichotomous, as relative, not absolute. All teaching systems will have some flexibility in each dimension. A high level of flexibility in every dimension is extremely difficult to achieve. Economy, scarce resources and rigid educational regulations often inhibit flexible teaching systems. With regard to cooperative learning, one may also argue that one person's flexibility ends where another's begins, for example, that one person's time flexibility is another's time delay.

A pedagogical technique is a manner of accomplishing teaching objectives. The techniques introduced here are organised according to the four communication paradigms used in computer-mediated communication. First, the techniques classified as one-alone are characterised by retrieval of information from online resources and the fact that a student can perform the learning task without communication with the teacher or other students. Second, the techniques classified as one-to-one can be conducted via e-mail applications. Third, the techniques discussed as one-to-many will typically be conducted via World Wide Web, bulletin boards or distribution lists for e-mail. Finally, the techniques presented as many-to-many can be organised within computer conferencing systems, bulletin board systems, or distribution lists for e-mail.

E-LEARNING TOOLS

Today, online education is part of the new educational culture. It has its own characteristics, and is filling a niche for many students that otherwise would not be able to attend classes. Numerous colleges and universities throughout in the world, are establishing distance education programs. Online instruction requires interpersonal communication.

Technology is just a tool, and tools are intended to be used for the benefit of humankind, meaning that the humans must control the tools and not the other way around. This defensive didactic diatribe negatively rejects the use of new tools, even though these thoughts do not represent the thinking of a majority of teachers. It elevates pedagogy over andragogy, that is, the professors refer to disciplines and training and who is in charge of the classroom and who has possession of the students.

Today, online education is part of a new culture with many distinct characteristics. It fills a necessary niche in the changing role of education. Without online education, many adult students with full-time jobs and families would never have the time to continue their studies. Online instruction, however, from the instructors standpoint, can be significantly more difficult than instruction in a traditional class.

Tools Used for Developing e-learning	Weighted Score
Document Creation Tools (e.g., PowerPoint and Word Processing)	85
Web Development Tools (e.g., Dreamweaver or FrontPage)	71
Learning Specific Authoring Tools (e.g., Authorware or Toolbook)	52
Programming Tools (e.g., Visual Basic, C++)	47
Authoring within a Learning Management System (e.g., Blackboard or Learning Space)	38

In a traditional classroom, it is the instructor's task, the first day of class to engage the students, and capture their attention, and excite the students for the coming semester. In an online class, this needs to be done through the course description. A well-designed outline needs to generate energy and excitement to motivate students to want to learn. In a traditional class, students read the required course material first, listen to the instructor's lecture, take notes, and ask questions if they have any. The lecture has to be stimulating and informative.

In a traditional classroom, the instructor is the actor and the classroom is his (her) stage. (S)he performs for the students, hopefully engaging them for the period of time they are in the class and motivating them to continue the pursuit of knowledge outside the class. In an online class, the instructor's "stand-up" lecture is replaced by notes. The lecture notes therefore need to be both stimulating and informative thereby replacing the instructor. To do this, standard outlines of course materials or PowerPoint presentations are boring, repetitive and likely will not hold a student's interest for too long. Having students nod off after reading a page or two of notes would indicate the presentation was not too interesting. Rather, there needs to be a mix of media within the outline. In a traditional classroom, the quality of the lecture depends significantly on the instructor, for example, the mood of the instructor, how they are feeling, time pressures to get through the material, and outside distractions in the class.

Even though pressures exist in an online environment, students in an online class can control and manage their study time and attention to the lectures at their own pace. By adding a mix of delivery media in the lecture notes, the instructor is adding diversity to keep a students attention and to allow for logical breaks in the students study time. However, in an online class, there is no body language or eye contact with the students as there is in a traditional classroom.

In an online class, students and faculty rely on the written word. If communication is sterile, students will be intimidated. Since the student's initial experience in the virtual classroom often determines his (her) future success, communication needs to be open, friendly, and responsive. Humour can warm up an otherwise cold and sterile delivery environment. It can bring the instructor and the students together in such a way as to create a positive learning experience.

The World-Wide Web (or the Web) is one of the most accessible tools available for academics to use. It allows an easy means of publishing material, it has a low learning-curve, the majority of its browsers are graphical and user-friendly, and above all it is free to most people in higher education. The premise being that students need access to greater resources to draw upon for their learning, or research, and that technology can achieve this goal.

The web can be viewed as one enormous resource that is interlinked, but ever expanding. The problem then is not so much the lack of resources, but more that of locating them, the needle in the pile of needles. Two approaches to solving this problem have developed over the years. The first is the use of gateways, the second the use of search engines.

Gateways are not the only way of locating existing web pages, but they do provide the advantage of being subject-specific and selective. However, it is possible that the Gateways in existence do not cover your subject area in any great detail. Furthermore, the topic you are interested in may be interdisciplinary and thus primary research and teaching resources may be located elsewhere. Either way, at some point you will want to look at an Internet Search Engine. Internet Search Engines have existed since the early days of the web.

Before moving on to looking at the types of things academics are using the web for in teaching, it is useful to confront some of the common problems users of the web encounter. The web works under a hypertext metaphor, i.e., it operates via a series of nodes and links. A user can be browsing a piece of information, and when they see a link they can simply activate it and some other node of information will be retrieved.

The web offers various opportunities for the academic who wishes to mount pedagogical material via the internet. The first stages of web design are very similar to designing any hypertext system. Start with the first 'node' of information and then consider what that should link to. If you are designing a site to *teach a skill* so that the student enters with an assumed knowledge base and exits having completed all of the tasks and having reached the teaching goal, you may favour a more linear design.

WEB-BASED LEARNING MODULES

The web-based learning modules can be used as homework for face-to-face classes, as the building blocks of distance education courses, and as stand-alone instructional units for public outreach. Web-based materials incorporate the latest in web design with interactive exercises, video, audio, and communication features and often meet high standards of instructional and graphic web design.

The faculty who create such modules learn quickly that designing and assessing their value can be challenging, requiring skill in instructional and graphic design, programming, and assessment of learning outcomes. Understanding the benefits of the web can help instructors decide if producing web-based materials is worth the effort.

Remote access is the primary incentive driving web-based instruction.

Web-based learning materials are a convenient alternative for students who cannot or do not want to take face-to-face classes, go to the lab during open hours, or attend a recitation in person. However, the realities of users' hardware can make assigning web-based materials problematic. Websites with complex graphics or large video or audio files can cause painfully slow downloads on computers with 56K or slower modems.

The web users are impatient, waiting 10 seconds or less before they lose interest in a website. Before building a site, make sure that the end user will be able to easily access the site given your anticipated technical design. Easy access to information is an integral part of web-based technology, as users are immediately linked to uptodate digital libraries, online publications, and more. Access can also mean exposure to authentic, real-world information not easily available through other sources. The web can present video, audio, and animated materials as well as give programmed feedback for user-entered responses.

The web-based materials can be regularly updated or revised. Java applets can be used to create complicated interactive learning materials; easy-to-use freeware for creating interactive assessments is available on the web. For those deciding to use any of these capabilities, the cost of development, greater download times, and more complex hardware capability must weighed against the benefit for the student. The overarching concern about the use of more complicated programming is whether the outcome of using a particular type of software actually helps a student achieve the learning objective of a lesson. Some web-based lessons allow students to choose which instruction they receive, making more individualised learning possible.

Student control is especially desirable for lessons that cover a wide range of difficulty so that students can enter and exit the lesson at an appropriate difficulty level, and is also important for skill-building exercises so that students can repeat a lesson until it is learned. While student control is often seen as desirable, it also means the instructor must relinquish some control of how students use materials. E-mail and bulletin boards built into learning modules allow students to respond to each other and the instructor, giving people the opportunity to revise and reflect upon their work. E-mail can also enable collaboration among students from different schools, states, nationalities, and ethnic and socio-economic backgrounds.

Now, many web modules are used in hybrid contexts, as students in face-to-face classrooms work and communicate with each other online, either during or outside of class. Bulletin boards can remove discussions from classrooms or extend them, allowing students to communicate with each other at their own convenience and in a safe environment. They also make course dialogue both visible and permanent, as threaded discussions are archived and referenced by both students and faculty.

A web search provides familiarity with online resources such as databases, dictionaries, assessment tools, or other websites that can be linked to the site. Before linking to or borrowing from other sites, learn about the complexities of copyright. All learning materials contain philosophical assumptions about how students learn, and these assumption, are implemented in an instructional design. It is important that philosophical and design choices are conscious choices, yet in many cases these decisions happen by default as designers unconsciously translate and reproduce existing instructional methods used in books, other media, or in their classroom practice directly to their online lessons. Some important considerations for designing the core of a lesson are the following:

Intended use and audience

Class-linked websites are usually either supplements to class work, or substitutes for existing class material. Supplementary materials may be optional, providing for a more comprehensive understanding of class content, or required, such as exercises that allow for extra skill development. If, on the other hand, the lesson is used as a substitute for classwork and/or materials, web content should function as class material and equal or improve on the quality of existing materials and instruction. Outreach websites used by the general public face a different kind of scrutiny and planning than sites used by classes, departments, or campuses. These sites are meant to be used by a wide variety of people, and are designed to motivate and entertain as well as educate. Outreach sites should have a professional appearance and should be easy and enjoyable to use.

Large-scale curriculum efforts conduct surveys and interviews to learn if the planned lesson fit the needs of the projected users. For smaller scale projects, a needs assessment is a more informal effort: the instructor can talk with students, other instructors, and content experts about what they want from new lessons, how lessons fit with current class activities, and how projected lessons fit with recent trends or discoveries in a discipline.

Learning and performance objectives

Web-based learning materials are built around a learning goal, which can be as straightforward as students will learn the four bones of the knee or as complicated as students will have a comprehensive understanding of the factors leading to the great depression. In self-contained materials, the learning objective should be explicitly stated so that students will have a clear idea of what they will learn by the time they finish the lesson. Students also need to understand when they have achieved the learning objectives, so some way of letting them know when they are successful should also be built into the site. Stating the learning objective explicitly will also help outline the lesson and guide the development of assessments. Performance objectives are derived from learning objectives. These are clear statements about what students should know and be able to do at the end of a lesson stated in terms of empirical assessments or observations.

Instructional method/pedagogy

Much of modern instructional design is grounded in pedagogical theories emphasising inquiry-based, active, or problem-based learning. Developing learning materials on the web that are personally meaningful and which engage students in the active analysis, synthesis, and evaluation of information is challenging. Interactive, hands-on exercises or simulations embedded in websites are a step toward active learning. Active learning activities also include visiting websites with authentic contexts or sites that afford access to primary source documents. Electronic communication can also foster collaboration and distributed expertise by removing spatial and temporal barriers to collaboration, and by allowing access to common data sets. Some critics of the recent push for educational technology observe that many web-based lessons merely reproduce traditional instruction by emphasising the memorisation of content and its regurgitation on tests. "Gift-wrapping" is a common practice of professors who take written lecture material and post it on the web, but there is nothing about the web that forces instructors to present material in this manner.

Scaffolding

While students are learning independently, it is essential to build ways to access help with subject matter. Hypertext can link students to terms, definitions, explanations, and images. Help can be in the form of text, supplementary links, illustrations, or video/audio files and can be programmed so that they are always available, or delivered to students only after they make repeated attempts at an exercise.

Assessment online

Assessments are an excellent way to add interactivity to the site, keep students engaged and reinforce material through the movement of clicking typing, and dragging and dropping. When giving feedback, decide whether the students are told only "correct" or "try again" or if they are given more detailed responses. Feedback can include extended explanations of why specific answers are correct or incorrect, and assessment questions can also link back to the material in the lesson.

Web-based assessments are an appropriate way to provide instructors with a valid picture of what their students know. The two related issues for assessing students online are item type/assessment method and communication with the instructor.

Computers are good at automating multiple-choice, matching, and short fill-in-the-blank test items, but are usually not set up to grade essays and performance assessments. There is a relationship between item type and the kind of knowledge that can be validly assessed. Multiple-choice, matching, and short answer items are more suited to recognition, memorisation, and problems with clearly defined answers, while essays, performance assessments, and portfolios better assess higher-order thinking skills such as analysis and problem solving.

Clear instructions and navigation

Instructors often counter that students could stop and read the instructions, but people tend to scan, rather than read, what they find on the web. Developers find a way to force users to read the instructions, such as presenting a page with instructions which the user cannot skip and asking that they click an "ok" or other button to continue into the lesson. Another suggestion for improving both instructional design and website design is to include a site map or "concept map", so that students always know where they are in a lesson.

This allows students to move to various parts of the lesson with a click of the mouse, to visualise how different components of the lesson relate to each other, and to know when they are finished. Depending on the intended use of the lesson, time and money can be spent ensuring smooth usability. The crucial planning phase is skipped in web development and design choices are made "on the fly", or by default. This can cause wasted effort as programmers must later go back and fix poorly executed designs.

Weak planning can also mean that the content and the instructional design of the site are more heavily influenced by the programmer than by the content and instructional experts. Begin by creating an outline or map of the site. This can be easily done in a low-tech manner on a piece of butcher paper with movable "sticky notes" used to represent separate screens or even by tearing out pieces of notebook paper. Using this type of schematic, decisions can he made about what sections follow and/or link to each other. Next, draw a rough picture of each screen that will be included, indicating text and picture layout.

Finally, attach to the storyboard an "asset list", including and describing all text, image, video, or sounds and links to be included on each screen include the computer file names for all elements of the site. After the storyboarding is complete, review all the features of each page to be sure they are essential for student learning and not merely included to enhance graphic design.

Instructors using web-based materials as a substitution for existing material want to be sure that students learn at least as much with the new materials as with the old. In collaboration with faculty, we often compare groups of students who have learned the materials with different teaching methods, assigning different materials and methods to two groups of students, then giving both groups the same test and checking to see if test scores between the groups are significantly different.

Pre- and post-tests are the traditional method of gauging if students have reached a pre-determined objective. Performance assessments often give a more valid understanding of what students know and can do than traditional written tests. A more subtle concern with any type of comparison involves changes to curriculum arising from the use of technology. One reason instructors choose to use a multimedia environment, such as the web or CD-ROM, is because they think they can achieve a learning goal not possible using traditional methods.

The focus of today's schools is on helping students become skilled and critical thinkers, participating actively in society's development. Such skills can more easily be nurtured by incorporating instructional styles where students are partners in the teaching-learning process, and by having a curriculum that promotes the development of these skills. Changing to this approach of learning from the traditional teacher-centred instruction has become increasingly common in many colleges and schools. The internet provides students with confidence in learning. It is seen as an alternative to the teacher-directed learning environment by encouraging active learning.

The internet gives simulation of real-world settings as it allows students to visit those places while in class. Use of the internet can save time for other activities in class because the instructor can post materials online so that students can have access to them, and thus time that would have been used going through those materials in class can be used for other activities. Novice users often do not have an idea of how to use the internet, even with the help of search engines and directories. Although internet use in class has been to allow students access to information, quite often they get lost in the world of the internet only to end with irrelevant information.

Internet provides a rich resource of materials, while it also an alternative source of information for students. The students acquire materials and information from the internet for their projects. The internet gives students access to information on text, video, and audio, which they cannot obtain from the teacher or textbook.

The students also use the internet when the teacher is busy helping other students. For those who fear asking questions in class, the internet is a quiet, private replacement of the teacher. The internet also provide uptodate information for students and the teacher. Internet encourages independent learning by students. It is a learning aid that makes it possible for students to obtain online help for their projects by using tutorials found on the internet.

The teacher and the students agree that the internet gives students an in depth understanding of what they learn. Due to time constraints in class, students are given skeletal information requiring the students to turn to other sources of instruction and reference such as the internet for supplemental materials. Students state that the use of the internet to supplement instruction increase their understanding. The teacher and the students voice the belief that the internet motivates students in their learning. Internet also imposes negative influences on the learning of the students.

In the class, students waste time surfing the internet. Searching the internet does not mean using search engines or directories and simply getting information needed. It requires skills to get the right information with the least time possible. Students' time is also wasted when the internet becomes slow because the networked system cannot cope with many students online at the same time.

With the internet, there is no control. It is a free-for-all information source where anyone can publish online any time. This has the danger of having inappropriate and unreliable information posted. In using the internet, students copy materials whose reliability and credibility questionable. Students develop a dependency on the internet during the class.

Students turned to the internet for information rather than using the knowledge they already had, and regarded the internet as indispensable to their learning even when inappropriate. Internet has changed the instructional approach in the classroom. Traditionally, the teacher is supposed to teach with students listening. In this classroom, the students also contributed to the teaching.

Students are updating the teacher on new innovations on some of the technologies they are using as the class progresses. Internet has reduced interaction in class. Students' use of the internet has undermined the teachers' confidence, affecting the teacher's confidence in his own competency and skills. The teacher also fear that the students appears to know what he was teaching, and hence his role is not significant. Thus, the teacher's authoritative control of the class, which is witnessed in traditional classrooms, is challenged. Students who surf the web for long periods of time are not active participants in the class.

Such students rarely finish their in-class assignments on time. The teacher complains that these students come to his office when he has other commitments to make-up their assignments, or bring them to the next class meeting. Internet affects the instructional styles of the teacher and the students. As an important tool for teaching and source of knowledge for students, it has realigned the teacher-student relations.

Unlike the traditional class, where the teacher is the *de facto* head of the class as a source of knowledge, and controller of class activities, the internet has reduced the role and significance of the teacher in both perspectives mentioned. Students no longer feel that they have to rely entirely on the teacher when in class. The students and the teacher concur that there is need to control internet use in class.

The teacher indicate that the uncontrolled use of the internet would in the long run hurt the students instead of helping them. Internet use in the class is conducive for the classroom environment.

The internet is perhaps the greatest purveyor of cross-cultural communication and information transfer. However, satellites, wireline, and wireless networks, among others, are also tools leading the charge in developing borderless nations. But the last 20 years has also seen the networking of individuals within single locations. The local area network (LAN) has pushed the envelope of computer networking to the extreme. New standards are allowing even computer and other information appliances in offices or homes to be networked via wireless connections.

While certainly mobile, the traditional book remains a frustrating nuisance, especially if one has to lug around several books while travelling on business. The book, in its traditional form, remains an isolated island of information, can be, at times, constraining, and clearly is unable to connect to any other electronic devices. More and more of our educational technology is wired or connected in some fashion.

From computers, to video-conferencing, to CD-ROMs, to distance learning systems and yes, to the internet, the demands to have a connected network of educational mediums is a major drive today to fulfil traditional, non-traditional, and corporate education needs. While not a new concept altogether, the e-book, in its latest iteration, provides an interesting avenue in the quest for better education and better educational technology use.

The e-book, in its raw form, is nothing more than electronic text. The e-book reader is the vehicle that is garnering the lion's share of attention in the industry today. The development of HyperCard and hypertext technology provided the enabling software and tools to create electronic, interactive books. These books could be downloaded to a PC, where non-linear, random accessibility was possible. The problem was that since the electronic text was stored on the hard drive, the portability, unlike a hard or soft copy book, was very limited.

E-books are gathering attention, both from consumers and the computer and publishing industries. E-books are a reality today and will certainly be a part of our future. The e-book itself is a relatively small, hand-held device, that is today primarily a storage-and-display unit. E-books offer a variety of features and functions that turn it from newfangled electronic reader into a useful, educational technology.

Whether in a traditional classroom setting or distant, independent study, the book, or some form of printed instructional material, is almost always used. With e-books, not only can you store multiple texts, you also can electronically search and cross-reference within and outside of the text. This offers clear time-saving benefits for the students, particularly when coursework requires the analysis and synthesis of material from multiple textbooks.

The e-book also offers features and functions that not only save time or open up a "virtual" book library, but also a means of personal creativity. For example, e-books offer variable font size. Many e-books come with a stylus, allowing the reader to underline passages or scribble notes in the margin. This is ideal for the student who wants to capture key thoughts without having to "maim" a paper book. Furthermore, e-books offer the option of book marking pages by simply touching the page. Higher-end e-books come with full-colour, high-resolution displays. The book has been around significantly longer than any other medium used for education or training.

Even today, the book is a dominant part of the educational landscape; this is not going to change anytime soon. The book has, for hundreds of years, influenced the way we reason, imagine, invent, and yes, learn. However, in a world of the 'wired', the book arguably has a big shortcoming: It is not connected to anything else. This shortcoming limits the book as an educational technology. E-books can and do have the ability to connect to networks via built-in modem ports. The e-book can be docked to personal computers to further extend their networking capabilities.

REFERENCES

El-Tigi, M. A, & B. H. Khan, "Web-based learning resources", In B. H. Khan (Ed.), *Web-based training*, Englewood Cliffs, NJ: Educational Technology Publications, 2001.

Forsyth, I., *Teaching and Learning Materials and the Internet* (2nd ed.), London: Kogan Page, 1998.

Galusha, J. M., *Barriers to Learning in Distance Education, Interpersonal Computing and Technology*, 5(3-4), pp. 6-14, 1998.

Hiltz, S. R., *The Virtual Classroom: Initial Explorations of Computer-mediated Communication Systems as an Interactive Learning Space*, Newark, NJ: New Jersey Institute of Technology, 1985

Roberts, L., "A Transformation of Learning: Use of the NII for Education and Lifelong Learning", In D. P. Ely & B. B. Minor (eds.), *Educational Media and Technology Yearbook 1995 / 1996*, pp. 50-66, Englewood, CO: Libraries Unlimited, 1996.

7

Evaluation of Web Learning

In today's society, education is becoming a commodity. In many ways the idea of education as a commodity is shorthand for some profound changes taking place: changes within education that are occurring in response to changes in the student clientele. The global information infrastructure is part of the cause and also part of the response. There was a time, not so long ago, that a student went to college at age 18 or thereabouts, completed a degree in about four years, and went off to the world of work. He or she progressed through the ranks of a company, mastering new skills along the way.

Education becomes a routine part of the day-to-day environment at work or at home. It must be available when it is needed, under conditions that do not make learning, work, and home mutually exclusive factors. Within universities the amazing growth of distance learning programmes is largely a response to that fundamental requirement. There must be a common, transportable currency to certify the knowledge and skills acquired as a result of education programmes. The fundamental result is that higher education is moving away from the traditional schedules and processes of instruction, to an emphasis on student learning.

In the process, online programmes move from the periphery to the mainstream of university strategy. And at the same time, traditional measures of quality, such as classroom time and on-campus resources, need to be reconsidered. In an online culture where information exchanges are ubiquitous, we expect to see customer/student rating systems emerge. While online rating systems will be critical to help students match their needs to the levels of service offered by a particular institution, there will also be an ongoing issue of independent, informed assessments of the overall quality of an institution. This is critical both for the student and for the taxpayers or donors who subsidise the institution.

The fundamental measure of success is student achievement: compare student performance to the intended learning outcomes of the course. There is more to the problem than simply putting courses online. Institutions must assume that students will not be physically present on campus; therefore, a properly designed programme provides online availability of services like programme information, registration, secure payment, academic advising, timely intervention regarding student progress, bookstore services, and a help desk for ongoing technical support. Whether the university's programme is offered on a campus or around the world, the library is essential. Distance learning courses introduce new issues concerning faculty workload, compensation, and intellectual property rights.

EVALUATION OF WEB-BASED FLEXIBLE LEARNING

The online courses allow for interaction in both synchronous and asynchronous modes. That is, they allow for place and time independence. People can interact at their own time and have the flexibility to take courses without physically walking in the classroom. Due to its synchronous and asynchronous nature, computer-mediated communication (CMC) allows for self-paced learning and reflection. The real strength of CMC lies on the premises of constructivist epistemology. According to constructivism, knowledge does not exist external to the learner. Rather, individual learners construct their own meanings based on their prior experiences. Learning is a result of construction, collaboration, reflection, and negotiation within a rich context in which learning is situated.

In a more decentralised environment, such as those facilitated with CMC, students take control of the learning environment, pose questions, moderate discussions, and summarise results. One of the major disadvantages of text-based CMC is the lack of visual and audible cues during communication. Body language, facial expressions, gestures, and voice intonation are all excluded from such an environment. A simple face expression can often communicate so much more than any text message. The same expression said with two different voices, can also have different meanings. This lack of richness of communication is one of the major disadvantages of CMC.

Furthermore, the technologies involved in distance education require an established infrastructure for an educational institution in order to be able to use it effectively. Such an infrastructure can often be expensive and beyond the budget limits of several institutions. Educators are often intimidated by the technology because they lack the skills and knowledge necessary for developing and managing online environments.

Like in all instructional settings, every online course is unique, depending on its goal, content, audience, budget, and the like. Developing and delivering an online course requires teamwork. During the development of online courses revisions are always necessary. Therefore, allow plenty of time to plan and develop the course. Furthermore, there is the false assumption among educators that teaching online is easy and it does not require as much time as traditional instruction.

In distance education feedback is very important. Students need many opportunities for feedback on their assignments, discussion participation, and overall progress. Feedback needs to be personalised and addressed to the individual student's work. General feedback addressed to the class as a group is also advisable, but it is individual feedback that touches the student.

In addition, it is important to contact the students on a weekly basis to check if they are having any problems with the course, assignments, use of technology, and get their continuous feedback for improving the course.

Online environments that rely heavily on text-based communication lack the visual and audible cues present in traditional face-to-face classrooms. As a result, communication that takes place in such environments has often been criticised as lacking in richness. The online classroom, more than in the traditional classroom, requires a variety of methods for evaluating student learning.

In the traditional classroom there are several ways that the teacher can use to evaluate students. A confused face or a head nodding can communicate a lot to the teacher. Non-verbal communication is a big part of the evaluation process of the traditional face-to-face classroom. In the online, the teacher can only evaluate what she has access to. She does not have access to facial expressions, voice intonation, or body language. Therefore, a variety of methods are essential for evaluating students and educational programmes delivered online.

The new web-based technologies offer good prospects for implementing flexible delivery options. Not only do web-based learning solutions offer effective responses to requirements for efficient information transfer, they also offer powerful alternatives for obtaining effective learning outcomes. Coinciding with the implementation of flexible delivery methodologies has been the onset of the information technology revolution and the development of digital communications technologies, such as e-mail and the World Wide Web (WWW).

In the context of educational services, web-based communications technology is not only seen as offering a supplement for traditional delivery methodologies, but also as being capable of revolutionising distance teaching and bringing on-and off-campus teaching modes closer into alignment.

Good practice in web-based learning settings will be driven by teachers and/or designers paying attention to effective use of 'conversations'. As in traditional classrooms, good practice is more than just stringing together a variety of 'conversations' *per se*. It is important that practitioners understand that, like the teaching strategies adopted in traditional classrooms, 'conversations' need to be appropriate and linked to the learning outcomes they are seeking to achieve.

There was a high level of interest in the evaluation of web-based flexible learning amongst providers and teachers. Teacher-centred approaches are dominant in current offerings despite the great potential of web-based flexible learning to engage learners in problem-solving, responding to change and improvement through self-monitoring and self-reflection. The nature and frequency of interactions promoted through web-based programmes have the potential to support and enhance lifelong learning with an emphasis on learner-directed learning and adaptability. Instructional designers of web-based programs need to take advantage of the capabilities offered by technology in ensuring that content materials encourage rich 'conversational' interactions and that student self-directedness and reflection are encouraged.

The tools for the evaluation of web-based learning are of two types, those that assist in the gathering of data for evaluations and those that assist in the analysis and display of results. Email surveys facilitate an efficient means of gathering quantitative data about teachinglearning, which can then be analysed through cluster analysis and displayed using the snapshot graphing tools. The tools indicated are helpful in displaying the range and quality of learning activity and therefore assist in making judgements about the appropriateness of instructional design and teaching methods.

Web-based flexible learning can support the kinds of learning needed for the knowledge economy of the information society, such as lifelong learning, learner-directed learning, learning to learn, contextualised learning, customised learning, transformative learning, collaborative/cooperative learning and just-in-time learning. The 'conversational' nature of teaching and learning provides a useful way for course designers and teachers to conceptualise their practice. Such 'conversations' should be thought of as including exchanges other than just face-to-face, and so are inclusive of all types of interactions inherent in resource-based and web-based learning. For learners to achieve expertise, learning must be deep, conceptual and reflective, with strong links between concepts and practice.

Teachers need to fashion learning experiences and 'conversations', or combinations of 'conversations', which lead learners to expertise. This is similar to the ways in which teachers align their teaching strategies to the learning tasks at hand. In attempting to determine the effectiveness of alternative web-based flexible learning systems, there is a need to categorise and compare groups of users as well as to describe characteristics of interactions of individuals within the same system.

As the development of web-based flexible learning systems continues, it is important to develop appropriate evaluation tools. Such tools need to take account of how to document and analyse learner interactions with such systems. The tools must also take account of the fact that non-linearity and associativity can be represented in numerous ways, and accommodate the importance of both the knowledge representation and interface issues.

Web-based communications technology is not only seen to supplement traditional delivery methodologies, it is seen as being capable of revolutionising 'distance teaching' and bringing on and off-campus teaching modes closer into alignment. All education and training from compulsory through to post-compulsory and higher education sectors are potentially involved in the uptake of these technologies and share stakeholder interests in understanding the educational consequences of the implementation of web-based learning.

While digital technologies can afford access to an enormous volume of information, this does not in itself translate into learning; nor does it ensure the development of expertise required for workplaces in a state of change. New curriculum theories and tools for evaluation are called for to address this challenge. Such concepts and tools will integrate theories of learning, new understandings of the knowledge targets for learning, new approaches to promoting teaching and assessment and new techniques for evaluating web-based learning experiences.

In the 'knowledge economy', the post-industrial developments of the previous generation now extend beyond mere preference for service sector activities: they embrace massive efficiency gains generated by the digital revolution and translate into an economy driven by imperatives of knowledge production and processing. 'Knowledge workers' now need to be active lifelong learners in order to understand and embrace technological developments and respond to the human resource needs of a rapidly changing economy. Knowledge workers are expected to create new knowledge by accessing information from broad sources. Workers must develop 'executive' knowledge management skills. They need to select the kinds of knowledge relevant to work, make choices about how this knowledge can and should be generated, and implement strategies to contextualise general knowledge for more specific ends.

Digital technologies play a critical role in operationalising every facet of knowledge production. Mirroring changes in workplace requirements, new concepts for learning have also evolved. Underscoring these, arguably, has been the constructivist view of learning and knowledge development in which learning is not characteristised as information transfer. New learning concepts include:

i) lifelong learning
ii) learner-directed learning
iii) learning to learn
iv) contextualised learning

v) customised learning
vi) transformative learning
vi) collaborative/cooperative learning
vii) just-in-time learning

The need for lifelong leaning is driven by rapid changes in technology and work practices. A widespread response by institutions to such needs is to allow flexibility in entry points to courses and to create new pathways for cross-sectoral articulation. Furthermore, there is an increase in the diversity of courses to suit the needs of diverse learners.

A key principle of adult learning is to facilitate self-directed learning. In doing so, the teacher plays a support role as a resource, a facilitator and as a challenger, rather than as a director of learning. However, adults need to acquire the skills and dispositions for self-directed learning in order to become successful lifelong learners. Self-directed learning skills can be learned and are an essential part of lifelong learning. Learning to learn gives more control over the direction and pace of one's own learning. Learner-directed learning encourages teamwork such as that needed for systems operations in the workplace.

Vocational education and training (VET) reforms driven by competency-based training (CBT), have created a significant shift from mastery of knowledge to contextualised and experiential learning and skilling for the workplace. The integration of theory and practice that can be offered through CBT is attractive to employers. School-based VET and increased apprenticeship and traineeship opportunities further enhance relevant learning experiences for many learners seeking vocationally relevant outcomes.

Web-based learning offers further opportunities for flexible delivery when and where required. Fundamental to knowledge productivity through innovation is the ability to challenge existing paradigms in response to new knowledge and new environmental circumstances, as well as the ability to make continual incremental changes within a dominant paradigm, whether of a knowledge discipline, an institutional framework, or an organisational design of work processes.

Essential for transformative learning is:

i) understanding given information
ii) learning about learning that includes strategies for analysis
iii) learning the content to challenge and refine meaning.

The communicative capabilities of web-based learning can provide rich opportunities, not just for acquiring new ways of working and thinking, but also collaboration, challenge and reflection with others engaged in the same process.

Web-based technologies, and educational technologies in particular, can enhance collaborative and cooperative learning and work beyond a single faculty to multiple disciplines in a global village. Knowledge economy workers need a capacity to access information from diverse sources and modify, extend and develop current skills and understandings in response to demand. Mirroring this, educational institutions need to supply learning opportunities which meet emerging needs.

The biggest revolution in distance education in recent times has been the increased use of networked information and communication technologies that broaden the scope of flexibility offered for teaching and learning, not only in addressing 'when' and 'where' questions of flexibility but also questions of 'what', 'how' and 'why'. Indeed, such educational technologies now set the agenda for flexible delivery and flexible learning. Web-based technologies are perceived by many to support effective pedagogy that includes acquisition of knowledge and development of skills and attitudes for lifelong learning. These technological innovations are currently creating new possibilities for both teachers and learners.

EVALUATION OF VIRTUAL LEARNING ENVIRONMENTS

Since the early 1980s, academics have used e-mail to communicate with each other. However, it is only recently with the growth of the web and the explosion of the internet into popular culture, that many lecturers and academic departments have started to exploit the potential of these technologies and the sophisticated network infrastructure provided by super-JANET to enhance their teaching. Increasing numbers of teaching staff are beginning to put their lecture notes and reading lists on the web for students to browse and are communicating with students via the e-mail.

Course outlines are commonly published on departmental websites. Some university libraries have web-interfaces for searching, checking availability and reserving books. Conferencing software is used in some institutions to create online discussion groups amongst students. These simple innovations are only the beginning and it is not surprising that there has been a recent wave of interest amongst software developers and IT research groups within universities in exploring ways to further leverage technology in an educational context. The systems that have been developed as a consequence of this interest may be viewed as specialised GroupWare for education.

They are designed to integrate and build on established network technologies that have recently begun to be used separately as teaching and learning tools. These include conferencing software, e-mail, online resources, search engines and multimedia databases, video-conferencing, shared whiteboards and interactive simulations. Depending on the pedagogical orientation and intended educational market of the developers, these systems are collectively and variously known as online learning environments, learning management systems, collaborative learning software or virtual learning environments (VLEs).

All VLE systems currently available are based on a client-server architecture. In general the client is simply a web browser that is used to access HTML pages on the server. Users of a VLE are divided into two main classes: students and tutors. Whilst tutors have a similar view of the system to students they will usually have additional tools and privileges that allow them to add materials, create conferences and track students progress. In some cases students have an area for conversation that is private from the tutor's view. Typically the system will provide a structured means for the tutor to create the course outline. The course outline will provide hyperlinks to the course pages themselves. In a web-based system these will be simply HTML-pages containing the material relevant to that part of the course.

Another key feature of a learning environment is getting to know the other students on a course or for tutors to get some idea of students' backgrounds, interests and aspirations. Many systems incorporate a list of students enrolled on a course—perhaps with e-mail addresses. Even more useful is the inclusion of a homepage for each student. Some systems provide an easy-to-use front-end for homepage editing.

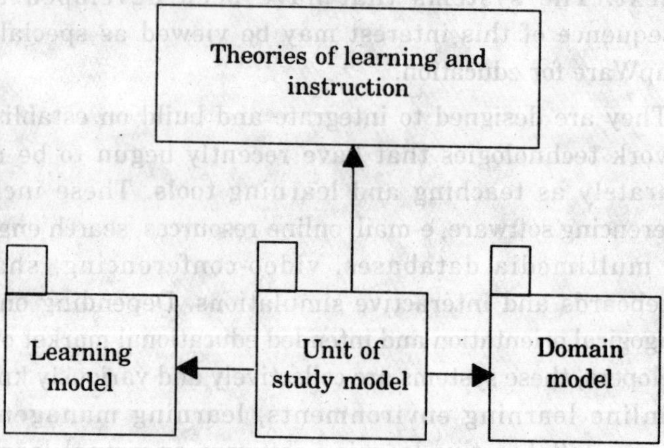

Figure 7.1: Packages of Pedagogical Metamodel

Most current VLEs incorporate some simple scheme for providing metadata about resources, course units and people, however several systems that are currently under development are paying more attention to the metadata issue. To be truly effective any metadata scheme should be standardised in some way so that it can be used across different systems rather than being local to a particular system. A VLE should allow tutors to create assignments for students to complete as they work through course material. It should provide a means for students to return completed assignments to the tutor for grading and feedback.

Some VLEs provide automated online quizzes for performing assessments, self-testing versions are also a feature of some systems. Synchronous collaboration tools such as Chat, Shared Whiteboards, Group browsing and videoconferencing are a feature of some but, by no means, the majority of VLEs. The relative importance of such tools in a system depends largely on the intended use of the system. One major advantage of VLEs is the ease with which multimedia resources can be accessed and stored within the learning environment as an integral part of the course package.

As more and more sophisticated educational materials such as interactive simulations get published online, the importance of multimedia facilities will increase dramatically. For truly interactive functionality students should not just be recipients of content uploaded onto the system by a tutor, but should be able to upload their own materials for other participants to look at. Some VLEs include a facility for students to build their own materials and objects they have found into the learning environment. A Calendar tool is a useful feature built into some VLEs.

Like search tools, a bookmarking facility can significantly decrease the amount of time spent navigating to frequently used places or items within the environment. Some systems include a more sophisticated version of bookmarking that allows participants to build up their own individual resource base.

Navigation is not strictly a feature or tool within a VLE, it is intrinsically part of the experience of using a VLE. The navigation facility allows a user to move around the environment, and the navigation model or metaphor in conjunction with the look-and-feel of the system is extremely important as it defines in many ways how the system is used. In addition to using hyperlinks and page to page browsing which are common to the experience of using a normal web browser, different VLEs will present the tools available and course structure in different ways.

The use of virtual learning environments and other online approaches to learning is still embryonic in many institutions. This may be expected to change rapidly if the high level of interest and awareness amongst educators about VLEs and alternative teaching / learning methods and the high rate of development of new and improved systems persists. Many advocates of VLEs within higher education are excited about their use because of their potential to allow a resource-based and student-centred approach to learning to be incorporated into their teaching.

One of the major blocks to adoption of this style of teaching and learning in universities is the extra time burden it places on tutors over the more traditional content-centred approach. Perhaps the key contribution that VLEs can offer is to allow a resource-based approach whilst also alleviating the tutor from an extra administrative burden. There are various ways that VLEs might achieve this but as yet there is currently no established evaluation methodology from a pedagogical perspective with which to assess different systems.

An integrated VLE implies that both staff and students are prepared to adopt an educational approach that is inherently more proactive from the students' perspective and that is in turn less pre-structured and more responsive to students' requirements from the teachers' perspective. Thus, first and foremost an evaluation framework needs to relate to the pedagogical process that the VLE is intended to support. Aside from these educational factors there are administrative and management concerns associated with adoption of an integrated VLE, which cannot and should not be ignored. There are two key considerations for VLE evaluation strategies:

i) VLEs should provide opportunities to improve the quality and variety of teaching and learning that are not being achieved using current methods.

ii) VLEs should reduce the administrative burden on teachers, thus allowing them to manage their workload more efficiently and to be able to give more time to individual students educational needs.

In 1993, Laurillard developed Conversational Framework, as an evaluation methodology for virtual learning environments. Laurillard's conversational model offers itself as an obvious and interesting candidate for providing the basis of a pedagogical evaluation framework for VLEs.

There are a number of key characteristics of the conversational model as applied to academic learning. These are drawn from Laurillard:

Discursive

i) Teacher's and student's conceptions should each be accessible to the other.

ii) Teacher and students must agree learning goals for the topic and task goals.

iii) The teacher must provide an environment within which students can act on, generate and receive feedback on descriptions appropriate to the topic goal.

Adaptive

i) The teacher has the responsibility to use the relationship between his own and the student's conception to determine the focus of the continuing dialogue.

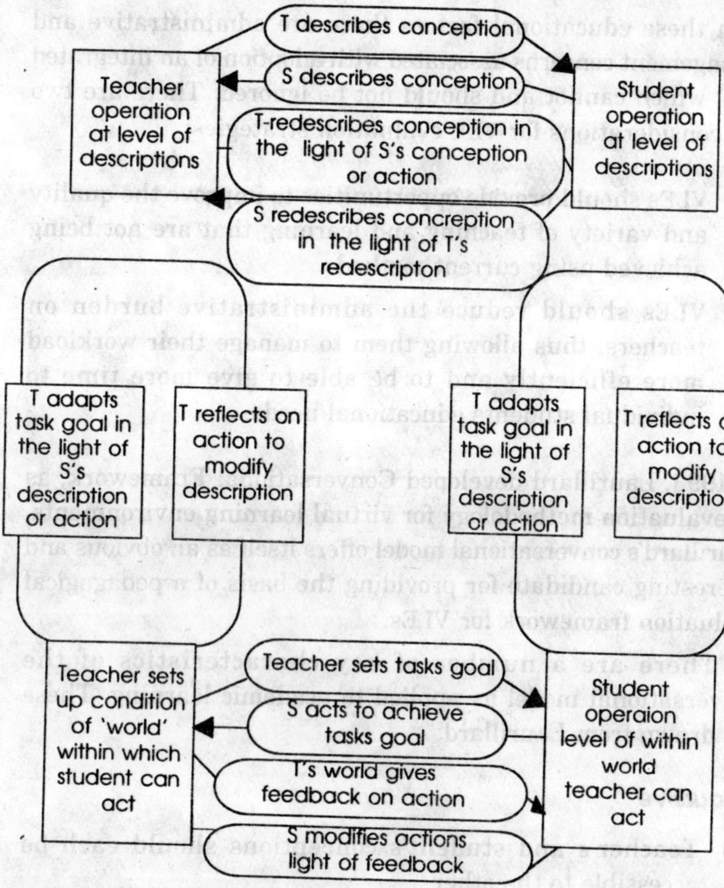

Figure 7.2: Conversational framework for virtual learning environments

Interactive

i) **The students must act to achieve the task goal.**

ii) **The teacher must provide meaningful intrinsic feedback on the actions that relate to the nature of the task goal.**

Reflective

i) The teacher must support the process in which students link the feedback on their actions to the topic goal for every level of d escription within the topic structure.

This simple framework offers much potential as a methodology for evaluating virtual learning environments. All interactions must be assumed to take place via the medium of the VLE. It is then possible to make judgements about how well the VLE handles each of the individual interactions labelled in the model.

The learning environment provides any extra tools to support reflection by the student on the relationship between the conversation at the level of descriptions and the activities they have completed or whether it provides structuring to assist the student in modifying their actions. The interactions illustrated in the model do not necessarily occur in the linear order given above and the model involves recurrence at several levels. In particular the conversation may shift freely between the conceptual level and the level of actions. Any software environment supporting learning should allow this to occur naturally.

For example, if e-mail is used as the tool for communication between tutor and student in a given VLE we need to know how the use of e-mail is embedded within the context of the dialogue about a specific topic or set of learning goals. In essence, the VLE provides the tools for a teacher to build a micro-world by allowing the teacher to construct learning activities enriched by multimedia resources and simulation programmes.

The crucial point from the perspective of the conversational framework is that the teacher should be able to construct the learning activity following a conversation with the student at the level of conceptions. A basic prerequisite for a VLE is that it should be interactive. It is not enough for material to be presented to a student and then be tested on it.

A VLE should allow the students to restructure the presented material, add resources of their own, annotate material, launch and run simulations, etc. In other words, the student should not merely be a passive observer of the 'micro-world' constructed by the teacher, but should be proactive in shaping the 'world'. A suitable evaluation framework for VLEs using the conversational model could be constructed in a variety of ways. VLEs is concerned with how to allow for the management of groups of learners. Formal teaching has a well evolved set of tools and approaches for dealing with groups of students en masse: these include lectures, seminars, tutorials and laboratory sessions. People are involved in the system in different roles—lecturers, postgraduate demonstrators, and personal tutors amongst others.

All of these mechanisms and people are integrated and organised by a timetable, which constrains how and when they can take place; and how they fit into a larger scenario involving many courses and demands on space and time. If VLEs are to be successful in enhancing educational quality, or if they are to achieve greater efficiency than traditional methods, they need to be able to address the types of issues that have previously been dealt with by the methods, techniques and tools outlined above. To be able to understand how they may attempt to do this requires some model that can generalise and explain these issues formally.

Formal education depends on organisations. Some have formal and independent status (e.g., universities), others are more notional (e.g., the education system). Some last for may years, others come and go (e.g., courses). Virtual Learning Environments represent both threats and opportunities for universities (and other educational establishments)—threats to traditional certainties, opportunities for increased effective-ness and efficiency. VLEs can be examined at two levels of recursion: the course level, and the institutional level. To date most VLEs have focused at the former, but increasingly they are being seen as providing institution wide solutions.

In the most traditional of approaches, coordination simply does not exist—students are not expected to work together in any way, and if they do, no provision is made for this. Those teachers that do support group learning usually structure this within existing lessons, and no provision is made for group assignments or other actions outside the timetabled sessions.

Students have always been able to use libraries to find additional materials to support their learning. This is perhaps what has ameliorated the lack of individual support offered by courses. However, guidance on how best to find what they need has always been in short supply. There is little evidence of any formal structures helping students to organise themselves into work or study groups.

While students may form study groups, neither time, space nor advice is provided for this, except in a few examples of study skills courses advising on group learning. Teachers can adapt their teaching to the needs of their learners, by changing the content of their lectures, the way they present them, and the supporting resources they use.

Formal teaching is designed to allow the teacher to treat the learner group as if they were one. However, the fact that the class does not consist of a single student constrains one key aspect—the ability of learners to engage in one to one conversations with the teacher. In a formal situation the conversational demands of a class of students would overwhelm the teacher, whereas if they had only one student, the balance between monologue and dialogue would most likely be very different. All these issues—resource negotiation, coordination, monitoring, adaptability, self organisation, and individualisation—can be affected by the use of technology.

EVALUATING WEBSITES

The technology for creating a website is relatively inexpensive and easily learned. Access to this information is worldwide, instantaneous, and increasingly available to more and more individuals. The web has the potential of becoming a great information equaliser, enabling anyone with a relatively small commitment of time and resources to make their message available to the world. Currently, there is almost no other area of technology development that is evolving more rapidly than web technology.

Large and small organisations, and many individuals, are scrambling to develop a presence on the web, competing for attention across an increasingly wide bandwidth. As the quality of presentation improves, the intensity of the competition among information providers increases. Each new wrinkle in technology development provides new challenges and opportunities for those who develop websites and provide information. It is surprising, given the importance of this technology and the resources that are being committed to implementing it, that there has been so little effort to date to evaluate it.

The technology is too important to ignore and the investments too large to go unexamined for very long. Despite the absence of concerted web evaluation efforts, we are clearly not starting from scratch. We have at least a half century of experience in evaluation and methods development. Much of the web evaluation that will be done will use familiar approaches, borrowing from other fields. But as with any new technology, these methods will have to be adapted and new strategies devised to address the unique phenomenon of the web. The methodological options that the website evaluator faces, because of the varied and complex nature of web technology, almost all evaluations will need to take a mixed-methods approach. One of the central challenges in mixed methods evaluation is how to integrate the results.

In many ways, a website provides an ideal context for evaluation. It is relatively easy to control and modify the content and presentation of material. It is possible to monitor user access very accurately. It is possible to use the site itself as the basis for gathering evaluation data. To provide a platform for exploring website evaluation, a website was designed and implemented.

The following are the typical purposes for websites:

i) *Information dissemination*: The most common use for a website is to make information available to anyone who would be interested in it. Organisations use websites to display their mission statements, organisational information, contact information, product information, directories, technical assistance, provide access to databases, and so on. Individuals use them to display their resumes, and information about their families, hobbies, or personal interests.

ii) *Education and training*: Although closely related to the information dissemination function, the web is often used to provide specific training in well-defined topical areas. In universities, websites are increasingly used to support specific course content. In organisational intranets, websites provide training in essential job functions.

iii) *Commerce and advertising*: The web is an ideal platform for advertising and purchasing products or services. Probably no area of web use will have a greater economic impact than this one.

iv) *Entertainment*: The web is a rich, interactive, graphical environment. Put simply, it is fun to use. It is not surprising that a variety of websites are constructed for entertainment purposes, to play games, post humorous essays or jokes, show cartoons, and so on.

v) *Communications*: The web has become a generic platform for communicating via the internet. Contemporary web technology allows the browser to send and receive e-mail, participate in bulletin boards and chat-room discussions, accomplish online conferencing using whiteboards and sometimes even two-way audio and video connections.

These purposes are the most frequent motivators for websites, most websites are designed to address more than one of them at a time. For instance, a corporate website is likely to be set up to disseminate information to the public, provide education and training, enable commerce and advertising, and facilitate communications.

Evaluation has traditionally been viewed as an activity that is conducted after the fact. Evaluaticn is more than simply "looking in the rearview mirror." There are two good reasons for this. First, evaluation has much to offer throughout the entire lifecycle of a programme. The methods that evaluators use and the perspectives they bring can greatly enhance the development of a product or programme. Second, even after the—fact evaluation will be hampered without intimate knowledge of the history and working of a programme. Understanding a programme in its developmental context is essential to understanding its effects and how those effects are produced.

Most website development is accomplished quickly under considerable time pressure. The desire to establish a presence on the web has become a compelling one for many organisations and individuals, rather than taking their time to "get it right", they prefer to "get it on" and fix it later. In many ways, website evaluation is no different from any other kind of evaluation. As in any programme or product development effort, there is a definable evaluand, multiple stakeholder groups that have a variety of sometimes conflicting interests, there are continual resource pressures, there are differences in goals and objectives, and so on. But in several important ways, website evaluation is a rather unique endeavor. Perhaps, the most notable is the key role of technology in the delivery of the site.

Concept mapping is a general method used to help groups to articulate a conceptual structure for any topic of interest. This can be used in a number of important ways in website evaluation. In the conceptualisation stage it provides a method for involving a broad range of stakeholders in mapping out the content for a website and determining the relative importance of different content areas. Using the related methodology of pattern matching, it is also possible to examine in detail the degree to which the various stakeholders are in consensus about the conceptual framework for the website. Concept mapping can also be an effective methodology for evaluating the expectations that users have for a website and, subsequently, determining how well those expectations have been met. Concept mapping can also be used as an organising methodology for analysing qualitative data.

Traditional survey methodology will also play an important role in website evaluation. Surveys can be used during the conceptualisation and development phases to conduct market research, identify potential users and ascertain their information needs and computer expertise. It can be conducted during the implementation and evaluation phases to asses user reactions to both the content and usability of the site. Experimental and quasi-experimental designs are the major tools evaluators. The web is a complex environment and evaluating it will necessarily be a complex endeavor. Since the web is a medium rather than just a message, it can be used in countless ways for a wide variety of purposes.

REFERENCES

Hiltz, S. R., "Evaluating the virtual classroom", In *Online Education: Perspectives on a New Environment*, ed. L. M. Harasim, 133-184. New York: Praeger, 1990.

Stubbs, S. T, and B. R. Burnham, "An Instrument for Evaluating the Potential Effectiveness of Electronic Distance Education Systems", *The American Journal of Distance Education* 4(3): 25-37, 1990.

Trochim, W., "An introduction to concept mapping for planning and evaluation", *A Special Issue of Evaluation and Program Planning*, 12, 1-16, 1989.

_______________ , "Concept mapping: Soft science or hard art?" *A Special Issue of Evaluation and Program Planning*, 12, 87-110, 1989.

8

Management of Web Education

The computer networks are the means of communication and becoming increasingly attractive for educators, as the price of modems and communication decreases, and as communication software slowly becomes easier to use.

The network seemed to provide a highly motivating context for learning, both for the students and for the teachers involved. The network serves as a source of ideas, suggested by students, teachers, or other adults elsewhere. The network provides an interactive environment, within which ideas can evolve through interaction.

The network provides a means for distributing various diverse tools for carrying out the project and also provides access to a diverse range of data, beyond that available at any one location. Perhaps most importantly, the network provides a wider and more diverse audience for the learning activity.

Student data collection, analyses and project write-ups are aimed not just for the teacher but also for a wider range of students, teachers, and other adults across the country or even around the world. Students' writing has been shown to improve when aimed at a wider audience provided by a network. In general, the network allows to use the diversity present in the world in powerful ways for education.

The network can provide support for learning, and now consider some of the ways that the class structure can provide support for network-based activities. The classroom activities that do not involve any electronic network, can have network activities outside the frame of a classroom. Students could participate after school, or during their free time even while at school. These observations on educational electronic networks can guide the exploration of the educational use of these networks. It is already clear that electronic networks are very good for conducting certain kinds of educational activities that would be very difficult in a conventional classroom. It is also clear that they are not suitable for all possible activities.

Since, 1990s, the practice of using electronic networks for instruction is becoming increasingly widespread. Since then, educationally-oriented electronic networks have continued to multiply, along with increasing numbers of teachers and students interested in finding ways to use these electronic networks as an instructional medium that can enhance motivation and learning.

However, number of instructional strategies are specific to particular instructional tasks and may not be applicable to all instructional tasks. Some of the common organisational elements can be employed to enhance the organisation of network-based activities, and thus to sketch out some of the strategies and tactics of successful educational networking.

Today, there are numerous electronic networks which enable schools to find partner schools and classes and to work together on instructional activities to accomplish various instructional goals. These networks are representative points on a continuum of possible approaches to successful project organisation, yet currently two of the three approaches appear as mutually exclusive options for network activity participants because of the "organisational framework" inherent in the activities promoted by that particular network.

Networks use even more obscure usernames, sometimes an arbitrary combination of letters and numbers. Usernames are essential for computers, but developing a working relationship with another individual is greatly facilitated by using people's names, since names are more meaningful to people. As more and more people begin to use electronic mail and conferencing, participants develop large groups of active correspondents.

For beginners, using electronic networks can be rather confusing. Even beyond the bits and bytes, beginning teacher-networkers want to know what this medium has to offer them and their students and how they can use the network to accomplish their instructional purposes. As they become more experienced in using networks, things become easier to accomplish. There are several reasons for this, but one reason is that through using the network a person is establishing a presence and is beginning to establish a reputation.

When people interact using an electronic network, information is flowing from those who have it to those who are seeking it. For this to work properly, those who have it must be willing to share it with those who need it. Thus, individuals who are willing to contribute as well as receive and who are willing to "hang in there" and work with the system over the long term will find that they build up a credibility which enables them to develop an extended group of professional colleagues who are willing to work with them to accomplish almost any task.

Most beginners tend to imagine that all of the other individuals working on electronic networks must be experts and their own inexperience makes them uncomfortable in asking about the experience level of others. In truth, most people using electronic networks are not experts. Very often they are people who possess a significant amount of enthusiasm, but considerably less technical expertise.

However, one should not automatically assume that others using the network are more, less or equally skilled as they themselves. This is important because in working with others, one should not assume, for example, that they know how to do a formatted file transfer or how to decompress a file. If they do not know how to do these things, then you will need to be prepared to share what you know in such a way that you will not overwhelm or threaten them.

There are number of specific strategies and tactics are have used in electronic network-based projects to facilitate their successful completion. Some of these techniques are useful across multiple stages of the project's lifecycle, however they are described into the lifecycle stages mentioned earlier: (a) proposal, (b) refinement, (c) organisation, (d) pursuit, (e) wrap-up, and (f) publication.

On many networks, one of the first problems that newcomers face is how to find willing participants for their own project activities. The usual method is for the newcomers to post a description of their projects on a public bulletin board for posting project proposals or to respond to someone else's project proposal.

There are number of management strategies used with great success in networking activities. A couple of important ones are the use of a timeline and distributed project ownership. There are a number of instances in electronic networking when timelines are not practical. An example of an instance in which timelines are not as important is when a new instructional activity is being developed and piloted for the first time.

In this case, it is often difficult to determine what comes next much less when it should happen in relation to the other aspects of the activity and how long it will take to accomplish. When using a timeline to help organise an electronic network-based instructional activity, it is best to build such a timeline with considerable allowance for changes and unforeseen circumstances. For a wide variety of reasons, it is quite difficult to achieve close coordination when working with large numbers of groups in different parts of the United States and around the world.

Many teachers are even more familiar with collaborative situations where there is a common lesson plan and all participants work through essentially the same sequence of events to arrive at essentially the same outcomes. A group of people working together on the network determine the key elements and general timeline for the project activity through joint agreement and that even then the specific teachers be encouraged to adapt the project in unique and individual ways to suit the needs of their particular situations.

In network-based activities that involve data collection, for example, once the data have been obtained and shared, there is no need for teachers to utilise the data in identical ways with their students. Instead, teachers can adapt specific procedures for utilising the data in ways most appropriate for their specific students. Network activities typically extend over longer time periods than classroom-based activities.

In the United States, more than half of the classrooms are wired to the internet and the number of classrooms connected is rapidly increasing. As this network infrastructure is put in place, teachers and learners can form and participate in network-based learning communities. But for these communities to function in productive ways we need to better understand how these communities are formed, grow, function in some mature steady state, and decline and terminate.

The network-based learning communities, formed around collaborative projects, and will present evidence for systematic patterns of change in these communities over time. Such communities are born, undergo growth, reach a level of mature functioning, and then undergo decline and cease to function. Like biological organisms, this lifecycle can be truncated when the community is not properly supported or when external factors intervene in some traumatic way.

There are different stages in the lifecycle of network-based community. There are five stages, or eight stages may turn out to be less important than the idea that learning communities go through a lifecycle, and that the nature of the interaction early on can be quite different from the nature of the interaction later. For learners and teachers to engage productively in these activities, it is important to understand the ways that these activities systematically unfold over time. An understanding of the lifecycle of network-based communities can lead to more productive learning by communities of learners distributed across the world.

The educational network interactions differ from other comparable face-to-face interactions in that the network interactions can be stretched out over time. The stages are:

i) group and task assignment,
ii) initiating problem solving,
iii) group discord and work obstacles,
iv) reorganisation, and
v) revival.

Student learning was affected by the different challenges over the lifecycle. Each challenge confronted students with similar problems and the application of conceptual knowledge in various contexts. The different challenges allowed students to discuss and write through a variety of genres including lists, narratives, and expository discourse. Over time, the solving of similar problems in different contexts allowed students to apply knowledge gained in earlier challenges to problems posed in later challenges.

Wrap-up activities took place inside the classrooms. These were sometimes reported on the network and sometimes they were not. There were two patterns of wrap-up activities. One type involved reflective activities in which students returned to ideas previously encountered during the project, discussed concepts, and presented their work. The other type was a teacher wrap-up. Unlike the elementary school classes, the middle school and high school students did not participate in reflective wrap-up activities. Wrap-up activity occurred primarily among the teachers. For the middle school teacher, this involved making sure all of the students had completed their work and had sent it over the network.

The high school teacher collected her students' ideas and composed a recreation design herself, and sent it to the network. However, network projects hold the potential for value to non-participating individuals and institutions. Distribution of knowledge gained through the project activity to a wider audience is the function of the publication stage. The construct of mediation in learning has been a central construct in socio-historical theories of learning. A new appearance in network-based learning environment, helpes to better understand its importance even in more familiar face-to-face learning environments.

IMPLEMENTATION E-LEARNING PLAN

In this new environment, individuals and organisations must continually acquire new skills and new ways of managing knowledge and information. As technology drives many of the revolutionary changes that are occurring in the work world, it also holds the potential of helping people and organisations keep pace with change. Technology, combined with e-learning can open the door to a learning revolution that could create an opportunity to increase individual and organisational productivity and efficiency for years to come.

E-learning is defined as instructional content or learning experiences delivered or enabled by electronic technologies (computer technology and the internet). E-learning content is delivered via electronic technologies with the intent to increase the workers' knowledge and skills so they can be more productive, find and keep high quality jobs, advance in their careers, and have a positive impact on the success of their employers, families and communities.

Implementing and deploying e-learning is not simply about converting traditional classroom training material into computer-based and web-based training platforms. Organisations must identify the skill gaps of their employees and design training materials that will assist in filling those skill gaps. Once skill gaps of employees have been identified, the organisation can then determine which training platforms have the opportunity to deliver the material effectively for each employee.

Conducting a skill gap analysis will determine whether training should be delivered via computer-based, web-based, classroom-based or combination of these training platforms. The appropriate method for delivering training should be based on the training needs of organisation's employees, not simply as a means to cut costs. Transitioning an organisation towards any type of e-learning platform should consider the following patterns:

i) Make learning a continuous and measurable process, not a one-time event;
ii) Make uptodate information instantly available to all users when and where they need it;
iii) Training should continuously assess the performance of both the information and all learners;
iv) Develop employees for greater responsibilities through skill-gap analysis;
v) Develop course content or use pre-existing courses;
vi) Publish content in all the formats needed for a complete training and development programme;
viii) Seamlessly support 'blended' training—the powerful combination of online and instructor-led courses proven to be the most efficient and effective way to train;
ix) Easily update and re-use information.

In order to determine if the organisation is ready for developing, deploying, and implementing e-learning, an organisational assessment is critical. The organisational assessment will identify four factors that must be reviewed. The four factors are:

i) Business objectives of the organisation
ii) Learning and performance analysis
iii) Technical needs analysis
iv) Stakeholder and readiness analysis

Deployment and development and of an effective e-learning solution must be uniquely tied to the business drivers of the organisation. Any successful e-learning initiative must be tied to specific results that an organisation seeks to achieve. Such results include increased profitability for a new product rollout, reduced time-to-market for a manufacturing branch, improved productivity, improved customer retention, or culture change as a result of a merger, acquisition or reorganisation. Understanding the specific learning and performance needs of all organisational stakeholder groups is essential to developing e-learning content that addresses and meets specific performance gaps and demands within the organisation.

Even when learning and performance needs cannot be resolved by training, the process of conducting needs analysis will determine the relevance of a given learning solution and provide a platform to begin the development of a more appropriate learning solution for a particular need.

Technical issues that must be analysed include functional requirements, integration requirements, information and network security needs, and data and reporting needs. Understanding these specific technical restraints that the organisation and the users will confront with e-learning is essential to ensuring e-learning success..

Multiple stakeholder groups most likely exist in any organisation and could be segmented based on job level, role, geography or other factors. It is important to determine the readiness of stakeholders in order to engage their efforts. This not only involves assessing the technical and subject matter skill level of employees, but also their receptiveness to e-learning versus learning in an instructor lead environment.

The implementation e-learning plan must address the issues identified in the business analysis, learning and performance analysis, technical needs analysis and stakeholder readiness analysis. The implementation plan will address the following items:

i) Learning and performance strategy
ii) Content strategy
iii) Technical strategy
iv) Readiness building
v) Roles, responsibilities, and accountability
vi) Capabilities strategy
vii) Processes, systems and structures strategy
viii) Communications strategy
ix) Measurement strategy.

Learning and performance strategy will focus on making learning a process, rather than a one-time hit or miss event. Often this incorporates a mix of instructor-led or face-to-face learning, web-based training, performance support, knowledge management, learner communities, and other learning tools. By ensuring that the learning and performance strategy specifically targets an organisation's business objectives, the greater the odds of achieving the results the organisation wishes to seek by implementing e-learning.

It is also important to identify the learning paths to determine how employees will proceed through the curriculum. This can provide a personalised roadmap so they are able to achieve the needed performance in the organisation. This is especially true since individuals within any organisation have very different needs regarding how they learn.

Design standards and high level instructional strategies should be established to ensure that content is engaging, high in quality, and consistent throughout all learning programmes. If employees are taking courses that do not have a similar look and feel, or overall instructional framework, the learning strategy may seem disjointed, be disjointed and be difficult for them to follow.

Global content standards ensure consistency and make the development and updating processes much easier. The content strategy should also determine what existing content should be migrated into the various formats (web-based, computer-based, instructor-based, etc., what new content should be developed, and what off-the-shelf content should be purchased. Instructional design principles of course content should incorporate problem solving, use scenario-based exercises, process-focused and the material presented should be relevant to their business activity.

The technical strategy is essential to meeting the organisation's high level functional needs. This includes the overall architecture for the e-learning solution that will be tailored to the specific functional requirements, current infrastructure, integration requirements with enterprise and other systems, and the overall learning strategy. It is essential to analyse and comprehend issues such as security, data needs, technical constraints, hardware and bandwidth issues, and any other matters that will affect the learning solution. In order to ensure that the technology solution meets the organisation's needs, this high level strategy will help to ensure that all customisation and integration is developed properly. As well, a system's performance—or lack thereof—may have a major impact on the success of an e-learning experience. Time lost while waiting for pages to load contributes to the feeling that e-learning is less effective than live instruction.

Readiness for e-learning begins with the creation of a team dedicated to developing a coherent vision of a successful e-learning initiative. It should be a cross functional team, made up of line executives, human resources, training and development and information systems personnel. Their mission is to develop a focused, aligned vision of how e-learning will meet specific needs and fit into their unique organisation. This step of ensuring buy-in and commitment from multiple stakeholder groups is vital to a successful implementation. Readiness among all in the organisation can be built in several ways, including regular communication, and special events to educate employees about new methods for deploying training.

If the e-learning is only available at the workplace, employees often complain of too many distractions and disruptions while trying to concentrate on course material. Breaking the material into small modules that can be completed in short periods of time will allow the learners to get through the material. In addition, learners will have questions and will want someway to get answers.

A successful implementation of any e-learning platform is ensuring that executive and upper management sponsorship exists. This includes establishing an oversight team, which should consist of the same individual involved in developing the e-learning vision.

When an e-learning initiative is being implemented, employees may need to develop new sets of skills and behaviours. If segments of employees are not familiar with the use of computers, browsers, and other widely used software applications, there will most likely be a need to develop an online or instructor-led course to provide them with the skills they need to use e-learning effectively. This will help to mitigate the risk of developing and deploying an e-learning solution and expecting all employees to use it, only to find that particular groups of employees do not have the basic computer skills.

An e-learning solution is often part of a larger effort to develop a learning-oriented organisation. This usually means employees are called on to be more proactive, self-directed learners. Competencies and skill gap analyses may be implemented that are unfamiliar to learners. In order to address these issues, the organisation may want to develop coaching techniques, workshops, or other ways to encourage a new set of behaviours associated with e-learning. Implementing a new e-learning strategy solution often means changing processes within an organisation. These processes may be related to administration, scheduling, delivering, managing, or developing learning in an organisation.

The new processes often must be realigned to match the new ways of learning, or match the functionality of the learning management system. By designing a plan to realign or change these processes before implementation, the organisation is more prepared for a smooth transition to the new e-Learning structure.

E-LEARNING MANAGEMENT SYSTEM

At present, e-learning platforms are organised into three fundamental macro components: a Learning Management System (LMS), a Learning Content Management System (LCMS) and a Set of Tools for distributing training contents and for providing interaction. The LMS integrates all the aspects for managing online teaching activities. The LCMS offers services that allow to manage contents while paying particular attention to their creation, importation and exportation.

The set of tools represents all the services that manage teaching processes and interactions among users. A Learning Content Management System includes all the functions enabling creation, description, importation or exportation of contents as well as their reuse and sharing. Contents are generally organised into independent containers, called learning objects, able to satisfy one or more didactic goals.

An advanced LCMS must be able to store interactions between the user and each learning object, aiming at gathering detailed information about their utilisation and efficacy. A good LCMS should accurately choose the contents to be offered to the student during the lessons as well as the way in which they must be provided. The importance of LCMS is related to the growing distance learning request that is determining a significant increase in content production.

The current effort is to avoid a useless duplication of contents by realising learning objects consonant to given standards in order to reuse them in different contexts and platforms. All the contents must be appropriately stored in special repositories and be easily accessible and updatable. In fact, a LCMS must be designed so as to enable a constant updating of its contents, allowing this process to semi-automatically take place.

Contents are not considered as objects external to the platform but as integral parts of it. This is possible thanks to the services that constitute the learning content management system. The trend towards a growing of training resources, though necessary to better characterise the training process, does not allow the teacher an easy consultation and use of these ones. At the same time, such an important number of resources can disorientate students that may run the risk of not choosing, during the auto-training phase, the contents more suitable to them.

Some information will support the content so as to better identify the domain in which resources are included and to draw LCMS and teacher's attention to the most peculiar characteristics of the training content. In literature, this descriptive process is known as metadata. At present, the scientific community and industries engaged in this field are trying to define standard metadata rules, so as to encourage understanding of the real semantic content of the various training resources.

The Learning Management System (LMS) embraces all the services for managing online teaching activities. A LMS must offer services able to evaluate and report the acquired skills storing the training path followed by them. A LMS should give the teacher the possibility of verifying the right formulation of the various lessons and suggesting changes in the learning path. Therefore, the functionalities of a LMS integrated within a distance learning platform can be so synthesised:

i) Student management
ii) Course management
iii) Student skill assessment

iv) Student activity monitoring and tracking
v) Activity reporting.

A student management system integrated within a LMS must manage a database containing standardised descriptions of student data so as to better identify the user and his characteristics. This type of description is generally based on dialects of the XML metalanguage (Extensible Markup Language), an element that guarantees data portability. An LMS must implement a functionality that adds a significant value to the distance learning process. This functionality is that enabling the student to consult, at any time, results he has reached and, consequently, to monitor his/her preparation level.

As for course management, an LMS can generally manage self-paced, asychronous introductor-led and sychronous instructor-led courses. Self-placed courses are usually asychronous, in hypertectual format, and give much freedom to the student who accesses a course index. The LMS system manages these courses starting from their creation. Asynchronous courses are run by an instructor, but they do not foresee interactive moments between students and instructor. Their design foresees delivery of strongly multimedia-oriented contents. Synchronous courses generally make use of collaborative learning, that is of all the tools that allow to create interactions in real time between students and instructor.

The efficiency of online training is related to the services made by the delivery platform as well as to their usage easiness. The services should satisfy teacher and student needs and it is therefore necessary that the same kinds of services are different in accordance with the user. In particular, teachers should be provided with tools enabling them to manage teaching processes for single individuals or groups, as well as all the interactions, including asynchronous discussions or live events. In addition, it is important to provide the teacher with updated reports on learner or learner groups' progresses so as to better manage evaluation processes and facilitate activities.

Virtual classroom service is a service designed for distributing courses in a synchronous mode, and also for supporting online live teaching. This type of service aims to reproduce the mechanisms present in a classroom during a traditional training session and is considered as a kind of container in which all the services able to recreate a virtual classroom atmosphere will be included. The use of a virtual classroom is obviously foreseen during "live" lessons in order to better manage synchronous interactions.

The transmitting network videoconferencing has been implemented through the introduction of compressing movie techniques that allow to reduce the use of band during the transmission in comparison with the uncompressed movies, intelligibility being equal. However, it is true that compressed video stream representations do not generally guarantee high definition movie reproductions. The latter can be anyway obtained by using high capability transmitting channels, whose utilisation can be more expensive.

Chat is the another sychornous communication within the e-learning platform. The chat service allows participants to send textual messages to the other students or the teacher in a public mode or a private one. Chat service surely increases collaboration within the environment in which it is used, but its utilisation must be continuously monitored by the teacher or tutor, since it could lead to a lack of attention and confusion within the virtual classroom.

The whiteboard has been one of the first services made available by an online learning platform. This service makes it available and shareable to teachers and learners a virtual space, usually called whiteboard. Both teachers and learners can work with it by virtue of control rights. This tool allows to write and draw on a shared space and to display such presentations as those realised by using the Microsoft PowerPoint software.

E-mail has been one of the first asynchronous communication tools used by e-learning environments. Students can send messages to a specific addressee only by having his e-mail address. Some platforms can include, within their own infrastructures, functionalities for exchanging e-mail messages, but most of them allow the integration with tools developed just for this purpose.

An online learning platform can be characterised through an analysis that takes into account:

i) the adopted methodologies;
ii) the level of the training path personalisation;
iii) operative modalities and didactic interaction quality;
iv) learning assessment and student tracking methods;
v) typology and quality of both didactic material and support system.

In the distance learning process, the student should be allowed to fully benefit from auto-learning, auto-motivation and auto-evaluation methods, and at the same time tutor and teachers should be provided with a direct and constant contact with the learners. So distance learning platforms must adopt a pedagogical approach based on constructivism theory.

Constructivist learning is based on students' active participation in problem-solving and critical thinking regarding a learning activity which they find relevant and engaging. They are "constructing" their own knowledge by testing ideas and approaches based on their prior knowledge and experience, applying these to a new situation, and integrating the new knowledge gained with preexisting intellectual constructs. Online learning platforms can implement easily a constructivist approach.

An online learning platform must be able to efficiently and effectively manage the single components of the process and their interactions. A distance learning platform that has these characteristics must carry out four principal functions: communication, information sharing, information access and cooperation. These functionalities characterise both the pedagogical and technological approach. As for technical requisites, the best solution to be adopted in platform design should be based on the utilisation of a multilayered, web-based architecture.

In particular an e-learning platform must be web-based, in this way the client can access the environment by simply using a web browser, without compelling the user to install other software into his computer. This characteristic should be always taken into account by industries producing distance training environments. Students only need a basic knowledge in informatics enabling them to interact with a browser, which also avoids difficult installations of proprietary software.

Another technical requisite to be considered is portability, that is, the possibility for a platform to rightly work independently of the computer and the operating system on which it runs. Obviously, the possibility of not installing proprietary software into the client machine increases system portability, since it guarantees that all clients can use the same services.

Such operations are surely speeded up by adopting descriptive standards, even when an intelligent tutoring system (ITS) is not used. Another aspect to be evaluated is related to the services integrated into the LMS and LCMS. As for management, services able to manage enrolments, training paths, and student tracking are really significant and add a new value. Platforms including such systems are surely ahead of others in services, as these tools will represent in the next future the core of an e-learning environment.

MANAGEMENT TOOLS

Web-based course management tools integrate technological and pedagogical features of the internet and the World Wide Web into a single, template-based authoring system to facilitate the design, development, delivery and management of web-based courses and online learning environments. Web-based course management tools include instructor tools, learner tools, and technical administration tools allowing for different types of users and for multiple internet and web-based activities embedded within the tool itself. Web-based course management tools incorporate various technological and pedagogical features including: Web links, search engines, synchronous and asynchronous communication, course announcement areas, student posting areas, tracking of student records and interactions, management of course information, and web-based development capabilities, among others. The purpose is to provide a central location for delivery of course content, related information or links, provision of models of assignments, communication between instructors and students, and group process for development of shared projects, as well as development of web-based products. This management tools have evolved over the last decade based on technological and pedagogical innovations from authoring bounded, programme-controlled learning systems such as Computer-Based Instruction (CBI) to authoring unbounded, learner-centred environments such as Web-Based Instruction (WBI).

From a technological perspective, the internet has revolutionised teacher-to-learner and learner-to-learner communication by making these interactions time and place independent through the use of email, discussion boards, and other internet-based technologies that facilitate asynchronous learning and information delivery.

Currently, WebCt has two editions, WebCt 3.5 standard edition and WebCt 3.5 Campus edition. The Campus edition offers a total online learning solution to institutions that wish to integrate their online courses with campus wide portals and student information systems. The Standard Edition is ideal for institutions that want a robust, pedagogically sound course platform, but do not need extensive features for enhanced scaling or integration with campus systems. In addition to facilitating the organisation of course material on the Web, WebCT also provides a variety of tools for instruction.

Table 8.1. Web-based instruction tools

Category	*General features*	*Instructional products*
Web-based Authoring Tools Examples include: FrontPage, Dream Weaver, Claris Homepage, Home-site, PageMil	-Browser interface -Utilised with internet-based technologies -Open system -Extensible -Dynamic content -Enables active/collaborative media -Require a steep learning curve in order to take full advantage of their features -Used by a variety of users to develop web sites for multiple purposes -Do not have specific instructor or learner tools	-Single web pages and integrated websites for the purposes of information presentation to support classroom instruction -Structured web sites resulting in a variety of formats for WBI -Personal and institutional homepages -Web publishing -Organisation of web-based resources -Complex animations and interactions when used with high level scripting languages (Java, Javascript, C++) and other web development tools
Web-based Course Management Tools Examples include: WebCt, Blackboard,TopClass, Virtual-U, Lotus Learning Space, Web Mentor, Symposium, TopClass, Convene, Embanet, Real Education, eCollege, E-Web, Internet Classroom Assistant, Softarc's FirstClass, Serf, Virtual-U, and Eduprise.com.	-Browser interface -Utilised with internet-based technologies -Open system -Easy to use -Dynamic content -Have specific tools for instructors, learners and administrators -Embedded communication tools -Used primarily to manage and deliver online learning in educational institutions and online training in corporate settings	-Online learning (e-learning) -Distance education programmes -Courseware (WBI) -Knowledge networks -Knowledge portals -Asynchronous & synchronous learning environments -Distributed learning environments

Blackboard offers three levels of its online development software, a free course creation tool which includes features such as content organisation, class discussions, group communication tools, online quizzes tool, electronic mail, an announcements posting area, and a digital dropbox among others; Blackboard 5, a more comprehensive e-learning software that includes customisable institution-wide portals, online campus communities, and an advanced architecture allowing easy integration of multiple administrative systems in addition to a course management system; and Blackboard CampusWide, which allows institutions to manage student registration and accounts, process financial transactions, and control everything from facility access to user identification.

TopClass provides a virtual environment to manage all aspects of content and class management and to deliver a flexible learning environment built upon web standards. It includes features such as security, online registration and enrolment, collaborative tools, a testing engine, student progress tracking, content and user searching, summary reporting, and course assembly tools that are platform independent.

Virtual-U is an online learning application made up of various integrated components. These include the VGroups conferencing system which gives instructors the ability to easily set up collaborative groups and define structures, tasks and objectives; course structuring tools which enable instructors to create complete courses online without programming knowledge; student performance tracking; and system administration tools.

WebMentor is a training environment for developing, administering, and delivering web-based training over the internet, intranets, and extranets. The browser-based authoring system supports course authoring and editing. The delivery system supports video and audio from local storage such as a CD-ROM; a customisable interface; large courses with many lessons; individualised instruction; and a flexible, multi-level lesson structure. WebMentor also includes support for administration, assessment, reporting, collaboration, and documentation.

Web-based course management tools now include such features and components under an integrated structure. The WWW has also changed the nature of instructional content and resources from a well-defined and stable knowledge base to an unfiltered and dynamic information base. CD-ROM-based authoring tools have commonly relied on stable content to organise and structure instruction which is why the resulting learning system is typically bounded and programme-centred. Web-based course management tools now include features and components that allow instructors and learners to modify content and contribute resources resulting in flexible and active information structures. From a pedagogical perspective, this means more flexibility in the design of WBI.

A strict instructivist approach typically results in a web-based course that has a tutorial structure in which the content is organised by the instructor and delivered or imparted to the students; and a radical constructivist approach typically results in a more learner-centred pedagogy where students use web features as tools to construct their own knowledge representations by restructuring content and creating and contributing their own resources to the course structure. It is more likely therefore that courses initially designed for traditional learning environments and later transformed to a web-based format using a web-based course management tool will undergo a pedagogical reengineering that is more constructivist and less instructivist in nature.

The critical factor that could impact the pedagogical use of authoring tools is whether the learner is perceived as the user or producer of hypermedia learning environments. The activities of the learner are regarded as the central focus in an educational context then learners should be thought of as software producers rather than software users in the development of educational software for both bounded CD-ROM titles and unbounded web-based resources. They propose the integration of learner tools that allow users for example to organise information in a meaningful way by positioning elements on the screen, creating new links, and generating multimedia objects.

Such cognitive tools could include a notebook to copy, edit and format text; a visual graphics tool to create marker buttons that point to multimedia elements such as video, audio, or pictures and enable the learner to manipulate those elements; and a cognitive mapping tool allowing flexible information representation.

Systems in an organisation may need to change to help promote learning in an organisation. These systems may mean an immediate feedback loop, rewards or incentives, annual reviews, competencies or others. There may be a need to alter some of these systems in order to encourage behaviour changes of employees or other stakeholders. Changing systems within an organisation to help encourage the new learning culture will take creativity.

The communications strategy announcing the deployment of an e-learning initiative should target the right message to the right stakeholder groups, using the most appropriate channels, and at the most suitable times. Communicating the deployment of a new e-learning initiative in a few organisation-wide emails and the organisation newsletter will not create the kind of awareness and buy-in that is needed to ensure successful deployment. There are usually many different and disparate groups within organisations that will need to be communicated with. These include all learner groups, executives, human resources, information technology personnel, advisory team, and external stakeholder groups that need to be "in the know" regarding the initiative.

A successful e-learning initiative must have a clear measurement plan in place. By establishing a measurement strategy, they can ensure continuous improvement and also measure the results that they have set out to achieve.

Qualitative tools measuring the learner's satisfaction with e-learning include learners' feedback about the course which may provide insight into how well the course was developed and what needs to be done to improve for the next time. Although the learner's may like the content, it is the impact on business that will determine its effectiveness.

REFERENCES

Gagne, R., L. Briggs, & W. Wager, *Principles of instructional design* (4th Ed.) , Fort Worth, TX: HBJ College, 1992.

Gibbons, A. S., & P. G. Fairweather, *Computer-based instruction: design and development* Englewood Cliffs, NJ: Educational Technology Publications, 1998.

Greeno, J. G, A. Collins, B. Beranek, & L. B. Resnick, "Cognition and Learning", In D. Berliner & R. Calfee (eds.), *Handbook of educational psychology*. 1-51, 1994.

Mayrhauser, A.V., *Software Engineering Methods and Management*, Boston: Academic Press, 1990.

Norrie, D.H., and B. R. Gaines, "The learning web: An agent-oriented network supporting knowledge access, collaboration and simulation", Proceedings of ED-MEDIA'95 : World Conference on Educational Multimedia and Hypermedia. pp.500-505, Charlottesville, VA: Association for the Advancement of Computing in Education, 1995

Royce, W.W., "Managing the development of large software systems: Concepts and techniques", Proceedings of the Nineteenth Annual IEEE WESCON Convention, 1970.

Snow, R. E., "Theory construction for research on teaching", In R. M. W. Travers (ed.), *Second handbook of research on teaching*, Chicago: Rand McNally, 1971.

Bibliography

Bellcore, "Guide for Multiplatform Graphical User Interfaces", LP-R13, Issue 2, December 1994.

Boud, D J., "Problem-based learning in perspective", in Boud, D J (ed) *Problem-Based Learning in Education for the Professions*, Sydney: Higher Education Research and Development Society of Australasia, 1985.

Burge, E. J, and J. M, Roberts, *Classrooms with a Difference: A Practical Guide to the Use of Conferencing Technologies*, Toronto: Distance Learning Office, Ontario Institute for Studies in Education, 1993.

______________ , and N. M, Carter, "It's Building, But Is It Designing? Constructing Internet-Based Learning Environments", Paper presented at the 18th World Conference of the International Council for Distance Education, University Park, PA, June 2-6, 1997.

Cahoon, B., "Teaching and Learning Internet Skills", In *Adult Learning and the Internet*, edited by B. Cahoon, pp. 5-13, *New Directions for Adult and Continuing Education*, no. 78, San Francisco: Jossey-Bass, 1998.

Davie, L. E, and Wells, R., "Empowering the learner through computer-mediated communication", *The American Journal of Distance Education*, 5(1):15-23, 1991.

El-Tigi, M. A, & B. H. Khan, "Web-based learning resources", In B. H. Khan (Ed.), *Web-based training*, Englewood Cliffs, NJ: Educational Technology Publications, 2001.

Engel, C E., "Not Just a Method But a Way of Learning", in Boud D and Feletti, G (eds) *The Challenge of Problem Based Learning*. London: Kogan Page, 1991.

Forsyth, I., *Teaching and Learning Materials and the Internet* (2nd ed.), London: Kogan Page, 1998.

Gagne, R., L. Briggs, & W. Wager, *Principles of instructional design* (4th Ed.) , Fort Worth, TX: HBJ College, 1992.

Galusha, J. M., *Barriers to Learning in Distance Education, Interpersonal Computing and Technology*, 5(3-4), pp. 6-14, 1998.

Gibbons, A. S., & P. G. Fairweather, *Computer-based instruction: design and development* Englewood Cliffs, NJ: Educational Technology Publications, 1998.

Greeno, J. G, A. Collins, B. Beranek, & L. B. Resnick, "Cognition and Learning", In D. Berliner & R. Calfee (eds.), *Handbook of educational psychology*. 1-51, 1994.

Gundry, J., "Understanding collaborative learning in networked organisations", *In Collaborative Learning through Computer Conferencing*: *The Najaden Papers*, ed A. R. Kaye, 167-178, Berlin: Springer-Verlag, 1992.

Harasim, L., "On-line education: A new domain", In *Mindweave: Communications, Computers, and Distance Education*, eds., R. Mason and A. Kaye, 50-62, Oxford: Pergamon Press, 1989.

_______________ , "Teaching and learning on-line: Issues in computer-mediated graduate courses", *Canadian Journal of Educational Communication*, 16(2):117-135, 1987.

Henri, F., "Distance education and computer-assisted communication", *Prospects* 18(1):85-90, 1988.

Hiltz, S. R., "Evaluating the virtual classroom", In *Online Education: Perspectives on a New Environment*, ed. L. M. Harasim, 133-184. New York: Praeger, 1990.

_______________ , and Turoff, M., "Structuring computer-mediated communication systems to avoid information overload", Communications of the ACM, 28(7):680-689, 1985.

_______________ , *The Virtual Classroom: Initial Explorations of Computer-mediated Communication Systems as an Interactive Learning Space*, Newark, NJ: New Jersey Institute of Technology, 1985

Horton, W., *The Icon Book: Visual Symbols for Computer Systems and Documentation*, NY, NY: John Wiley and Sons, Inc., 1994.

Johnson, E., "Teaching on international computer networks", *TEXT Technology* 3(2):3-5, 1993.

Kaye, A., "Computer-mediated communication and distance education", *In Mindweave: Communications, Computers, and Distance Education*, eds. R. Mason and A. Kaye, 3-21, Oxford: Pergamon Press, 1989.

Kearsley G, and Shneiderman, B., "Engagement theory: A framework for technology-based teaching and learning", *Educational Technology*, 38, 5 (September-October 1998), pp. 20-23.

Khan, B. H., "A framework for e-Learning", *e-learning magazine*, December 2001.

_______________ , "Discussion of resources and attributes of the Web for the creation of meaningful learning environments", *Cyber Psychology and Behaviour*, 3(1), 17-23, 2000.

Klemm W. R, and Snell, J. R., "Enriching Computer-Mediated Group Learning by Coupling Constructivism with Collaborative Learning", *Journal of Instructional Science and Technology*, 1, No2, 1996.

Knowles, M. S., *The Modern Practice of Adult Education, From Pedagogy to Andragogy*, New York: Cambridge, 1980.

Kristensen, T., "A Pedagogical network of schools in the Bergen region", In TeleTeaching, eds. G. Davies and B. Samways, 523-528, Proceedings of the IFIP TC3 Third Teleteaching Conference, *TeleTeaching* 93, Trondheim, Norway, 20-25 August, 1993.

Laurel, B., Ed., *The Art of Human-Computer Interface Design*, NY, NY: Addison-Wesley, 1990.

Mayrhauser, A.V., *Software Engineering Methods and Management*, Boston: Academic Press, 1990.

Microsoft Corporation, "Windows Interface Guidelines for Software Design", *The Microsoft Guidelines for designing a user interface for Windows-based applications*, Redmond, Washington: Microsoft Press, 1995.

Mullet, K., and D. Sano, "Designing Visual Interfaces - Communication Oriented Techniques", Englewood Cliffs, NJ: Prentice Hall, 1995.

Nielsen, J., E. M. D., Galdo, R. C. Sprung, and P. N. Sukaviriya, "Designing for International Use", *In Proceedings of ACM CHI '90 Conference on Human Factors in Computing Systems*, 1990.

Norrie, D.H., and B. R. Gaines, "The learning web: An agent-oriented network supporting knowledge access, collaboration and simulation", Proceedings of ED-MEDIA'95 : World Conference on Educational Multimedia and Hypermedia. pp.500-505, Charlottesville, VA: Association for the Advancement of Computing in Education, 1995

Paulsen, M.F., *The Online Report on Pedagogical Techniques for Computer-Mediated Communication*, 1995.

Phillips, G. M, Santoro, G. M, and Kuehn, S. A., "The use of computer-mediated communication in training students in group problem-solving and decision-making techniques", *The American Journal of Distance Education* 2(1):38-51, 1988.

Rapaport, M., *Computer Mediated Communications: Bulletin Boards, Computer Conferencing, Electronic Mail, and Information Retrieval*, New York: John Wiley & Sons, 1991.

Roberts, L., "A Transformation of Learning: Use of the NII for Education and Lifelong Learning", In D. P. Ely & B. B. Minor (eds.), *Educational Media and Technology Yearbook 1995 / 1996*, pp. 50-66, Englewood, CO: Libraries Unlimited, 1996.

Royce, W.W., "Managing the development of large scftware systems: Concepts and techniques", Proceedings of the Nineteenth Annual IEEE WESCON Convention, 1970.

Salasoo, A, E., White, T. Dayton, B. Burkhart, and R. Root, "Bellcore's User Centered Design Approach", In M. Wilkind Ed., Usability in Practice, Boston: Academic Press, 1994.

Snow, R. E., "Theory construction for research on teaching", In R. M. W. Travers (ed.), *Second handbook of research on teaching*, Chicago: Rand McNally, 1971.

Soloway, E, Jackson, S. L, Klien, J., et al., "Learning Theory in Practice: Case Studies of Learner Centered Design", (University of Michigan), 2000.

Special Issue of Evaluation and Program Planning, 12, 87-110, 1989.

Stubbs, S. T, and B. R. Burnham, "An Instrument for Evaluating the Potential Effectiveness of Electronic Distance Education Systems", *The American Journal of Distance Education* 4(3): 25-37, 1990.

Trochim, W., "Concept mapping: Soft science or hard art?" A

_______________ , "An introduction to concept mapping for planning and evaluation", *A Special Issue of Evaluation and Program Planning*, 12, 1-16, 1989.

Tufte, E. R., *The Visual Display of Quantitative Information*, Cheshire, Conn: Graphics Press, 1983.

Virzi, R. A., "Streamlining the Design Process: Running Fewer Subjects", *Proceedings of the Human Factors Society 34th Annual Meeting* (pp. 291-294), Santa Monica, CA: Human Factors Society, 1990.

Index